SERVICE OFFERING AGREEMENTS

AGREEMENTS

A Guide for ITIL® V3 Intermediate Exam Candidates

BCS THE CHARTERED INSTITUTE FOR IT

Our mission as BCS, The Chartered Institute for IT, is to enable the information society. We promote wider social and economic progress through the advancement of information technology, science and practice. We bring together industry, academics, practitioners and government to share knowledge, promote new thinking, inform the design of new curricula, shape public policy and inform the public.

Our vision is to be a world-class organisation for IT. Our 70,000 strong membership includes practitioners, businesses, academics and students in the UK and internationally. We deliver a range of professional development tools for practitioners and employees. A leading IT qualification body, we offer a range of widely recognised qualifications.

Further Information
BCS The Chartered Institute for IT,
First Floor, Block D,
North Star House, North Star Avenue,
Swindon, SN2 1FA, United Kingdom.
T +44 (0) 1793 417 424
F +44 (0) 1793 417 444
www.bcs.org/contactus

SERVICE OFFERINGS AND AGREEMENTS
A Guide for ITIL® V3 Intermediate Exam Candidates

Richard Griffiths

Published by British Informatics Society Limited (BISL), a wholly owned subsidiary of BCS The Chartered Institute for IT First Floor, Block D, North Star House, North Star Avenue, Swindon, SN2 1FA, UK.
www.bcs.org

ISBN 978-1-906124-60-1

British Cataloguing in Publication Data.
A CIP catalogue record for this book is available at the British Library.

Typeset by Lapiz Digital Services, Chennai, India.
Printed at CPI Antony Rowe Ltd, Chippenham, UK.

CONTENTS

FIGURES AND TABLES

AUTHOR

Richard Griffiths is an experienced and respected Service Management expert who has worked as a practitioner, trainer and consultant in all aspects of ITIL® for a number of organisations worldwide.

Richard has been a question compiler and senior examiner at every level for over 10 years and uses the knowledge gained from running many ITIL courses to tailor his writing to the audience of potential candidates and those who want to know more about how Service Offerings and Agreements are applicable to them in their organisations.

He is the co-author of *IT Service Management – A guide for ITIL® V3 Foundation Exam Candidates* by the same publisher.

ABBREVIATIONS

CMDB	Configuration Management Database
CMMI	Capability Maturity Model Integration
CMS	Configuration Management System
COBIT	Control Objectives for Information and related Technology
CSF	Critical Success Factor
CSI	Continual Service Improvement
EFQM	The European Foundation for Quality Management
ELS	Early Life Support
eSCM-SP	eSourcing Capability Model for Service Providers
ISO	International Organization for Standardization
IT	Information Technology
ITIL	IT Infrastructure Library
ITSM	IT Service Management
itSMF	IT Service Management Forum
KPI	Key Performance Indicator
MTBF	Mean Time Between Failures
MTBSI	Mean Time Between Service Incidents
OGC	Office of Government Commerce
OLA	Operational Level Agreement
PBA	Patterns of Business Activity
RACI	An example of an Authority Matrix: Responsible, Accountable, Consulted, Informed
ROI	Return on Investment
SD	Service Design
SIP	Service Improvement Plan

SKMS	Service Knowledge Management System
SLA	Service Level Agreement
SLM	Service Level Management
SLP	Service Level Package
SLR	Service Level Requirement
SO	Service Operation
SOX	Sarbannes–Oxley framework for corporate governance
SS	Service Strategy
ST	Service Transition
TCO	Total Cost of Ownership
UC	Underpinning Contract

GLOSSARY

Accounting   The process responsible for identifying actual Costs of delivering IT Services, comparing these with budgeted Costs, and managing variance from the Budget.

Best Practice   The proven Activities or Processes that have been successfully used by multiple organisations. ITIL is an example of Best Practice.

Budget   A list of all the money an organisation or business unit plans to receive, and plans to pay out, over a specified period of time.

Budgeting   The Activity of predicting and controlling the spending of money. Budgeting consists of a periodic negotiation cycle to set future Budgets (usually annual) and the day-to-day monitoring and adjusting of current Budgets.

Business Case   A justification for a significant item of expenditure. It includes information about Costs, benefits, options, risks and possible problems.

Business Relationship Management   The Process or Function responsible for maintaining a relationship with the business. Business Relationship Management usually includes:

- managing personal relationships with Business Managers;
- providing input to Service Portfolio Management;
- ensuring that the IT Service Provider is satisfying the business needs of the customers.

This Process has strong links with Service Level Management.

Business Service Management   The ongoing practice of governing, monitoring and reporting on IT and the Business Service it impacts.

Capabilities   The abilities of an organisation, person, Process, application, Configuration Item or IT Service to carry out an Activity. Capabilities are intangible assets of an organisation.

Capital Expenditure   The cost of purchasing something that will become a financial asset, for example computer equipment and buildings. The value of the asset is depreciated over multiple accounting periods.

Charging   The requirement for payment for IT Services. Charging for IT Services is optional, and many organisations choose to treat their IT Service Provider as a cost centre.

Contract   A legally binding agreement between two or more parties.

Cost   The amount of money spent on a specific Activity, IT Service or business unit. Costs consist of real cost (money), notional cost (such as people's time) and depreciation.

Cost–Benefit Analysis   An Activity that analyses and compares the costs and the benefits involved in one or more alternative courses of action.

Cost Effectiveness   A measure of the balance between the effectiveness and the Cost of a Service, Process or Activity. A cost-effective process is one that achieves its objectives at minimum cost.

Cost Type   The highest level of category to which costs are assigned in Budgeting and Accounting.

Critical Success Factor   Something that must happen if a Process, project, plan or IT Service is to succeed. Key Performance Indicators (KPIs) are used to measure the achievement of each Critical Success Factor. For example, a Critical Success Factor of 'protect IT Services when making changes' could be measured by KPIs such as 'percentage reduction of unsuccessful changes', 'percentage reduction in changes causing Incidents' etc.

Demand Management   Demand Management covers Activities that understand and influence customer demand for Services and the provision of capacity to meet these demands. At a strategic level Demand Management can involve analysis of Patterns of Business Activity and user profile. At a tactical level it can involve use of Differential Charging to encourage customers to use IT Services at less busy times.

Differential Charging   A technique that is used to support Demand Management by charging different amounts for the same IT Service Function at different times.

Direct Cost   The cost of providing an IT Service that can be allocated in full to a specific Customer, Cost Centre, Project etc. For example, the cost of providing non-shared servers or software licences.

External Service Provider   An IT Service Provider that is part of a different organisation to its customer. An IT Service Provider may have both internal customers and external customers.

Financial Management   Financial Management consists of the Function and Processes responsible for managing an IT Service Provider's Budgeting, Accounting and charging requirements.

Fixed Cost A cost that does not vary with IT Service usage. An example would be the cost of server hardware.

Function A team or group of people and the tools they use to carry out one or more Processes or Activities (e.g. the Service Desk or IT Operations).

Governance Ensures that policies and strategy are actually implemented, and that required processes are correctly followed. Governance includes defining roles and responsibilities, measuring and reporting, and taking actions to resolve any issues identified.

Indirect Cost That part of the Cost of producing an IT Service that cannot be allocated in full to a specific customer. For example, the cost of providing shared servers or software licences. An Indirect Cost is also known as an overhead.

ITIL® The IT Infrastructure Library (ITIL) is a set of best practice guidance for IT Service Management. ITIL is owned by the Office of Government Commerce (OGC) and consists of a series of publications giving guidance on the provision of quality IT Services, and on the processes and facilities needed to support them.

IT Service A Service provided to one or more customers by an IT Service Provider. An IT Service is based on the use of information technology and supports the customer's business processes. An IT Service is made up from a combination of people, processes and information technology and should be defined in a Service Level Agreement.

IT Service Management The implementation and management of quality IT Services that meet the needs of the business. IT Service Management is performed by IT Service Providers through an appropriate mix of people, processes and information technology.

IT Service Provider A Service Provider that provides IT Services to internal customers or external customers.

itSMF The IT Service Management Forum which operates as the independent ITIL user group worldwide.

Key Performance Indicator A metric that is used to help manage a Process, IT Service or an Activity. Many metrics may be measured but only the most important metrics are defined as Key Performance Indicators (KPIs) and are used to manage and report actively on the Process, IT Service or Activity. KPIs should be selected to ensure that efficiency, effectiveness and cost-effectiveness are all managed.

Lifecycle The Lifecycle is made up of the various stages in the life of an IT Service, Configuration Item, Incident, Problem, change etc. The Lifecycle defines the categories for status and the status transitions that are permitted. For example:

- The lifecycle of an application includes requirements, design, build, deploy, operate and optimise.

- The expanded Incident lifecycle includes detect, respond, diagnose, repair, recover and restore.

- The lifecycle of a server may include ordered, received, in test, live, disposed of etc.

Metric   Something that is measured and reported on to help manage a Process, IT Service or Activity.

Objective   The defined purpose or aim of a Process, an Activity or an organisation as a whole. Objectives are usually expressed as measurable targets. The term Objective is also informally used to mean a requirement.

Office of Government Commerce   The Office of Government Commerce owns the ITIL brand (copyright and trademark). Office of Government Commerce is a UK Government Department that supports the delivery of the government's procurement agenda through its work in collaborative procurement and in raising levels of procurement skills and capability within Departments. It also provides support for complex public sector projects.

Operational Cost   Cost resulting from running IT Services. These are often repeating payments. For example, staff costs, hardware maintenance and electricity (also known as current expenditure or revenue expenditure).

Operational Level Agreement (OLA)   An agreement between an IT Service Provider and another part of the same organisation. An OLA supports the IT Service Provider's delivery of IT Services to the customers. The OLA defines the goods or services to be provided and the responsibilities of both parties. For example, there could be an Operational Level Agreement:

- between the IT Service Provider and a procurement department to obtain in agreed times;

- between the Service Desk and a support group to provide Incident resolution in agreed times.

Partnership   A relationship between two organisations that involves closely working together for common goals or mutual benefit. The IT Service Provider should have a Partnership with the Business and with Third Parties who are critical to the delivery of IT Services.

Planning   An activity responsible for creating one or more plans. For example, Financial Management planning.

Practice   A way of working or a way in which work must be done. Practices can include Activities, Processes, Functions, standards and guidelines.

Pricing   The Activity for establishing how much customers will be charged.

Process   A structured set of Activities designed to accomplish a specific Objective. A Process takes one or more defined inputs and turns them into defined outputs.

A Process may include any of the roles, responsibilities, tools and management controls required to deliver the outputs reliably. A Process may define policies, standards, guidelines, activities and work instructions if they are needed.

Relationship   A connection or interaction between two people or things. In Business Relationship Management it is the interaction between the IT Service Provider and the business.

Resource   A generic term that includes IT infrastructure, people, money or anything else that might help to deliver an IT Service. Resources are considered to be assets of an organisation.

Return on Investment   A measurement of the expected benefit of an investment. In the simplest sense it is the net profit of an investment divided by the net worth of the assets invested in that investment.

Risk   The uncertainty of outcome, whether positive opportunity or negative threat. A Risk is a possible Event that could cause harm or loss, or affect the ability to achieve Objectives. A Risk is measured by the probability of a threat, the vulnerability of the asset to that threat, and the impact it would have if it occurred.

Role   A set of responsibilities, activities and authorities granted to a person or team. A Role is defined in a Process. One person or team may have multiple Roles (e.g. the Roles of Configuration Manager and Change Manager may be carried out by a single person).

Scope   The boundary or extent to which a Process, procedure, certification, contract etc. applies. For example, the scope of the Change Management Process may include all live IT Services and related Configuration Items, the scope of an ISO/IEC 20000 certificate may include all IT Services delivered out of a named data centre.

Service   A means of delivering value to customers by facilitating outcomes that customers want to achieve without the ownership of specific costs and risks.

Service Catalogue   A database or a structured document with information about all live IT Services, including those available for Deployment. The Service Catalogue is the only part of the Service Portfolio published to customers, and is used to support the sale and delivery of IT Services. The Service Catalogue includes information about deliverables, prices, contact points, ordering and request processes.

Service Hours   An agreed time period when a particular IT Service should be available. For example, 'Monday to Friday 8 a.m. to 5 p.m. except public holidays'. Service hours should be defined in a Service Level Agreement.

Service Improvement Plan (SIP)   A formal plan to implement improvements to a Process or IT Service.

Service Level   A measured and reported achievement against one or more Service Level Targets. The term Service Level is sometimes used informally to mean Service Level Target.

Service Level Agreement   ITIL defines a Service Level Agreement (SLA) as an agreement between an IT Service Provider and a customer. The SLA describes the IT Service, records Service Level Targets, and specifies the responsibilities for the IT Service Provider and the customer. A single SLA may cover multiple IT Services or multiple customers.

Service Level Management   The Process responsible for negotiating Service Level Agreements, and ensuring that these Service Level Agreements are met. Service Level Management is responsible for ensuring that all IT Service Management Processes, Operational Level Agreements and Underpinning Contracts are appropriate for the agreed Service Level Targets. Service Level Management monitors and reports on Service Levels, and holds regular reviews with customers.

Service Level Requirement   A customer requirement for an aspect of an IT Service. Service Level Requirements (SLRs) are based on business objectives and used to negotiate agreed Service Level Targets.

Service Level Target   A commitment that is documented in a Service Level Agreement. Service Level Targets are based on Service Level Requirements, and are needed to ensure that the IT Service Design is fit for purpose. Service Level Targets should be SMART, and are usually based on Key Performance Indicators.

Service Management   A set of specialised organisational capabilities for providing value to customers in the form of Services.

Service Management Lifecycle   An approach to IT Service Management that emphasises the importance of coordination and control across the various Functions, Processes and systems necessary to manage the full lifecycle of IT Services. The Service Management Lifecycle approach considers the strategy, design, transition, operations and continual service improvement of IT Services.

Service Manager   A manager who is responsible for managing the end-to-end lifecycle of one or more IT Services. The term Service Manager is also used to mean any manager within the IT Service Provider. The term Service Manager is most commonly used to refer to a Business Relationship Manager, a Process Manager, an Account Manager or a senior manager with responsibility for IT Services overall.

Service Portfolio Management   A dynamic method for governing investments in Service Management across the enterprise and managing them for value.

Service Reporting   The Process responsible for producing and delivering reports of achievement and trends against Service Levels. Service Reporting should agree the format, content and frequency of reports with customers.

SMART An acronym for helping to remember that targets in Service Level Agreements and project plans should be Specific, Measurable, Achievable, Relevant and Timely.

Supplier A third party responsible for supplying goods or services that are required to deliver IT Services. Examples of Supplier include commodity hardware and software vendors, network and telecom providers and outsourcing organisations.

Supplier and Contract Database A database or structured document used to manage supplier contracts throughout their lifecycle. The Supplier and Contract Database contains the key attributes of all contracts with Suppliers, and should be part of the Service Knowledge Management System.

Supplier Management The Process responsible for ensuring that all contracts with Suppliers support the needs of the business, and that all Suppliers meet their contractual commitments.

Supply Chain A Supply Chain is made up of the activities in a Value Chain that are carried out by Suppliers. A Supply Chain typically involves multiple Suppliers, each adding value to the product or service.

Support Hours The times or hours when support is available to the users. Typically these are the hours when the Service Desk is available. Support hours should be defined in a Service Level Agreement, and may be different from service hours. For example, service hours may be 24 hours a day, but support hours may be 7 a.m. to 7 p.m.

Third Party A person, group or business that is not part of the Service Level Agreement for an IT Service, but is required to ensure successful delivery of that IT Service. Examples of third parties include a software supplier, a hardware maintenance company or a facilities department. Requirements for third parties are typically specified in Underpinning Contracts or Operational Level Agreements.

Total Cost of Ownership A methodology used to help make investment decisions. Total Cost of Ownership assesses the full Lifecycle cost of owning a Configuration Item, not just the initial cost or purchase price.

Underpinning Contract A contract between an IT Service Provider and a third party. The third party provides goods or services that support delivery of an IT Service to a customer. The Underpinning Contract defines targets and responsibilities that are required to meet agreed Service Level Targets in a Service Level Agreement.

Utility The functionality offered by a product or service to meet a particular need. Utility is often summarised as 'what it does'.

Value Chain   A sequence of processes that creates a product or service that is of value to a customer. Each step of the sequence builds on the previous steps and contributes to the overall product or service.

Value for Money   An informal measure of Cost Effectiveness. Value for Money is often based on a comparison with the cost of alternatives.

Value Network   A web of relationships that generates tangible and intangible value through complex dynamic exchanges through two or more organisations. Value is generated through the exchange of knowledge, information, goods or services.

Variable Cost   A cost that depends on how much the IT Service is used, how many products are produced, the number and type of users, or something else that cannot be fixed in advance.

Warranty   A promise or guarantee that a product or service will meet its agreed requirements.

USEFUL WEBSITES

www.bcs.org/iseb	Information Systems Examination Board, British Computer Society
www.efqm.org	European Foundation for Quality Management
www.isaca.org	Information Systems Audit and Control Association
www.iso.org	International Organization for Standardization
www.isoiec20000certification.com	ISO/IEC 20000 certification and qualification schemes
www.itil-officialsite.com	The official ITIL website
www.itsmf.co.uk	The IT Service Management Forum
www.itsmfi.org	itSMF International
www.ogc.gov.uk	Office of Government Commerce
www.sei.cmu.edu/cmmi/	Carnegie Mellon University Capability and Maturity Model

PREFACE

This book has unique value in that it covers the topics of Service Offerings and Agreements in detail embodying the author's knowledge and experience in these areas. The concepts are explained in an easy-to-understand manner that is free of technical jargon. More complex areas are broken down into smaller understandable sections.

The relevant sections of the core ITIL books are fully explained at a level that enables comprehension, application and analysis to take place. This is important as the exam will test at these levels of learning. The syllabus for Service Offerings and Agreements covers material in both the Service Strategy and the Service Design books. This publication brings everything together in one place.

The book is applicable for candidates studying for the Service Offerings and Agreements qualification or considering doing so. It is also useful for anybody looking for information on and an insight into the processes of:

- Service Portfolio Management
- Service Catalogue Management
- Service Level Management
- Supplier Management
- Demand Management
- Financial Management

SECTION 1:
INTRODUCTION

The concepts and terminology of the Service Lifecycle are introduced and the role of Service Offerings and Agreements within the Lifecycle are discussed in this section.

Service Management is all about ensuring that the Services provided are aligned to the needs of the business areas and that these Services are supported throughout their operation. Service Management is able to fulfil this role by using the Service Lifecycle and a number of processes.

1 THE CONCEPT OF SERVICE MANAGEMENT AS A PRACTICE

Main book references: SS 2.1, SD 2.1

It is important to understand exactly what Service Management is and how it is used by organisations to deliver and manage their Services. ITIL defines a Service as follows:

SERVICE

A Service is a means of delivering value to customers by facilitating outcomes that customers want to achieve without the ownership of specific costs and risks.

The outcomes are the drivers for purchasing the Service in the first place. They are what the customer wants to receive or achieve. For example, when ordering an item from an online seller, the customer wants to receive a specific item at an agreed price within certain timescales. From the customer's point of view, the value of a particular Service is determined by how well the outcomes are delivered.

The specific costs and risks of the Service are not owned by the customer. The customer is gaining value by achieving their desired outcomes while the costs and risks are held by the provider of the Service (i.e. all the infrastructure, people and processes required to deliver the Service). The customer does not own the costs and risks of providing the Service; they just want their outcomes and value.

Within organisations, Services are sourced from internal areas (e.g. IT, Human Resources or Facilities Management). These areas have the necessary knowledge and experience to own and manage the costs and risks specific to their areas.

Service Management brings together Processes and Functions to deliver Service.

SERVICE MANAGEMENT

Service Management is a set of specialised organisational capabilities for providing value to Customers in the form of Services.

The customers of a Service are concerned with outcomes and value while Service Management is there to coordinate and manage Resources in order to deliver those outcomes and value. The Resources are coordinated and managed through the utilisation of Processes and Functions.

A simple everyday transaction or service would be obtaining money from a bank. The customer is only interested in achieving their outcome of obtaining money. The speed and ease of the transaction will provide the value. The availability of ATMs (Automated Teller Machines) allows customers to access money. As customers, their sole interest is in the money being dispensed quickly and securely, they are not interested in the mechanics of how the money is dispensed or the infrastructure that allows it. In the short space of time that the customer is using the ATM (and the shorter the better for the customer (value)), any number of network links and database access activities are being utilised. The ATM has been purchased, located and loaded with money; again this is not what the customer is interested in. While the customer concentrates on outcomes and value, it is Service Management that pulls everything together to facilitate the delivery of the service. Service Management is responsible for managing and coordinating all the Processes and all the internal and external areas of the bank, in this example, that allow or enable the service to be delivered.

The specialised organisational capabilities in the definition of Service Management are Processes, Activities, Functions and Roles utilised by a Service Provider when delivering a Service. It is not just the Processes, Activities, Functions and Roles, but also the management and organisational structures that are put in place around them.

Historically, IT departments may have tended to be fragmented and operated in 'stovepipes' concentrating on their part of a Service without having visibility of the Service as a whole. For example, it would have been commonplace for the Networks area to lack a clear picture of exactly what traffic was moving across the Network and how important each piece was to the business areas. Service Management brings a holistic approach pulling together the different areas to ensure focus on the delivery of Service. Previously, the individual cost of components that make up a Service were understood, but perhaps not the overall cost of the Service in a way that was recognisable to the customer. Also, there would have been different definitions and perceptions of a Service depending on whether you were a customer, a component area or an IT Manager.

One of the key roles of Service Management is to understand the Service perspectives of both the customers and the providers and to act as the bridge or translation between the two. In order to facilitate this, Service Management has to understand the value of each Service to customers and, by extension, their relative importance. Services need to be 'fit for purpose' and Service Management must ensure that it gives the outcomes that the customers want to achieve. Service Management also manages the costs and risks involved with the provision of a Service.

The capabilities of Service Management are moulded by the intangible nature of service output. In manufacturing, there is a real and visible output that can easily be checked and measured. This is not always the case with services. Another challenge is the close relationships and dependencies between service providers and the customers of the services.

As well as being a set of specialised organised capabilities, Service Management is also a professional practice. As with any professional practice, it is supported by shared common standards, skills and experience that are backed up by formal training programmes and recognised examinations.

There is a worldwide community of Service Management practitioners, in both the public and private sectors, who share best practice. Service Management was initially developed in government and large non-government organisations, particularly in the area of financial services. However, it has now been adopted in all sectors and by both large and small organisations. As more organisations have become involved in the delivery of services through growth, greater complexity and the increasing use of outsourcing and shared services, Service Management is being used by an ever growing number of companies. Organisations are attempting to maintain their performance in relation to competitors by using practices that are in common use.

PRACTICE

A Practice is a way of working or a way in which work must be done. Practices can include Activities, Processes, Functions, Standards and Guidelines.

Service Management as a professional practice strives to improve the levels of performance in managing services. This step improvement over time has led to the build up of Service Management intellectual capital and the emergence of best practice.

BEST PRACTICE

Best Practice is the proven Activities or Processes that have been successfully used by multiple Organisations. ITIL is an example of Best Practice.

Best practice is updated as better methods are developed and proven. Organisations are able to compare their performance against the results generated by using industry best practice. They can then gauge the level and amount of alterations required to their practice in order to bring them up to best practice.

For organisations or enterprises looking to improve how they operate, there are many sources of best practice. Figure 1.1 shows some of these sources, many of which are in the public domain.

Figure 1.1 Sources of best practice (Source: OGC ITIL Service Strategy ISBN 978-0-113310-45-6)

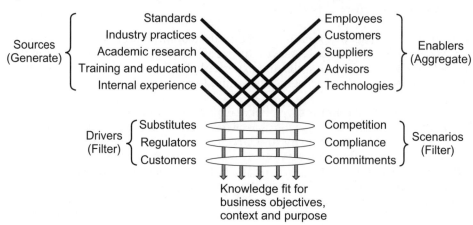

Proprietary knowledge must be relied on if sources available externally to the organisation are not used. This tends to be developed over time and by its nature is organisation specific and is often not documented.

On the other hand, knowledge of public frameworks tends to be more widely dispersed over a number of organisations. Public frameworks and standards have developed through validation across different organisations in different sectors and of differing scale. Industry knowledge is widespread and individuals with the knowledge can be recruited allowing the knowledge to be further spread. Training programmes and accompanying recognised certification also boost the spread of knowledge.

Organisations that have access to, and use, best practice are better placed than those organisations that do not. Proprietary knowledge alone is not enough. In fact proprietary knowledge should be seen as an addition once best practice has been incorporated.

ITIL is an example of best practice.

ITIL

The IT Infrastructure Library® (ITIL) is a set of best practice guidance for IT Service Management. ITIL is owned by the Office of Government Commerce (OGC) and consists of a series of publications giving guidance on the provision of quality IT Services, and on the processes and facilities needed to support them.

OFFICE OF GOVERNMENT COMMERCE (OGC)

The Office of Government Commerce owns the ITIL brand (copyright and trade-mark). Office of Government Commerce is a UK Government Department that

"IT Infrastructure Library® is a Registered Trademark of the Office of Government Commerce in the United Kingdom and other countries."

supports the delivery of the government's procurement agenda through its work in collaborative procurement and in raising levels of procurement skills and capability within Departments. It also provides support for complex public sector projects.

Organisations should not attempt to introduce ITIL as an 'off-the-shelf' solution. Instead, they should adopt and adapt the ITIL framework for their specific situation. In other words, they should not be looking to implement ITIL, rather they should be aiming to implement a Service Management solution based on the ITIL framework, which is relevant for the needs of their organisation.

In my experience, working as a Service Management consultant, I have seen a number of organisations who have successfully used ITIL to break down the traditional 'stovepipes' or 'islands' that existed between IT teams. However, I have also seen a few who have replaced the old non-communicating 'stovepipes' or 'islands' with ITIL process teams who now also act in isolation from the other teams. This is the risk of implementing ITIL without understanding the communication requirements and the need for 'joined-up' Service Management that does not lose sight of the business goals.

ITIL is a framework rather than a standard and is a source of good Service Management practice. For organisations that wish to acquire certification, then ISO/IEC 20000 is the appropriate standard to be assessed and audited against. ISO/IEC 20000 is the standard of IT Service Management (ITSM) and is aligned to ITIL.

IT SERVICE MANAGEMENT

IT Service Management is the implementation and management of quality IT Services that meet the needs of the business. IT Service Management is performed by IT Service Providers through an appropriate mix of people, Process and information technology.

The ITIL framework provides the knowledge that is key for achieving the standard certification. It is centred on what has to be achieved and ITIL gives clear guidance on how solutions can be developed. The International Organization for Standardization (ISO) and the Office of Government Commerce (OGC) have agreed to keep the standard and the framework as closely aligned as possible, although the different development lifecycles and the different purposes served mean that this will not always be completely possible. The close synchronisation between the standard and the framework is supported by the itSMF.

itSMF

The IT Service Management Forum which operates as the independent ITIL user group worldwide.

ITIL has two parts:

- The Library Core. This comprises five publications containing best practice guidance to all types of organisations involved in the provision of services to a business.
- The Library Complementary Guidance. This is a set of additional publications that are industry specific, organisational type specific, technology architecture specific and operating model specific.

The Library is able to provide guidance to all types of organisations that provide IT Services to businesses. This guidance is valid regardless of organisation size and complexity, and regardless of whether it is an internal service provider or an external service provider. The framework can be used and the guidance adapted for different environments with the Complementary Guidance advising on how the Core can be implemented in each.

The ITIL framework has evolved, to a large extent, over the last 20 years. It is seen at its best when implemented pragmatically and sensibly and where the business goals are not lost or forgotten. The first ITIL publications tended to be based on a single topic or function. The second iteration pulled many of the processes together in order to emphasise the 'joined up' nature of the framework. The most recent iteration (ITIL V3) is broader and still takes a holistic Service Lifecycle approach.

The five publications that make up the ITIL Core are:

- Service Strategy (SS) ISBN: 9780113310456
- Service Design (SD) ISBN: 9780113310470
- Service Transition (ST) ISBN: 9780113310487
- Service Operation (SO) ISBN: 9780113310463
- Continual Service Improvement (CSI) ISBN: 9780113310494

Each of these core areas is described in detail in their individual publications and they are viewed as being part of an overall Service Lifecycle (see Figure 1.2).

The Service Lifecycle approach allows coordination and control across the Processes, Functions and supporting tools required to manage IT Services. It takes into account the Strategy, Design, Transition, Operation and Continual Improvement of IT Services.

Service Strategy and Service Design cover the initial determination and refinement of business requirements followed by implementation in the Service Transition phase. Service Operation is responsible for the live operations, and improvement is covered by Continual Service Improvement. Opportunities for Continual Service Improvement occur during all the other four stages of the Service Lifecycle.

Figure 1.2 The Service Lifecycle (Source: OGC ITIL Service Strategy ISBN 978-0-113310-45-6)

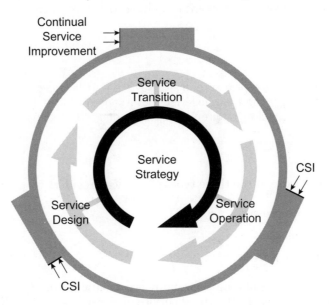

SERVICE STRATEGY

Service Strategy looks at individual services today and in the future, as well as incorporating the design, development and implementation of Service Management as a whole. The objective of Service Strategy is to provide better services (better than those previously provided and better than the competition). Competition and technology do not stand still, so Service Strategy has to evolve and develop continually. One of the key roles of Service Strategy within an organisation is to ensure that money is spent on areas that are important to the business. Costs, benefits and risks must be taken into account.

Understanding risk is particularly important in Service Strategy and throughout the whole Service Lifecycle.

RISK

Risk is defined as uncertainty of outcome, whether positive opportunity or negative threat. A Risk is a possible Event that could cause harm or loss, or affect the ability to achieve Objectives. A Risk is measured by the probability of a threat, the vulnerability of the asset to that threat, and the impact it would have if it occurred.

Successful organisations demonstrate effective risk management by using frameworks where risks are identified, analysed and reacted to with appropriate countermeasures. Risk management is an important part of governance.

GOVERNANCE

Governance ensures that policies and strategy are actually implemented, and that required processes are correctly followed. Governance includes defining roles and responsibilities, measuring and reporting, and taking actions to resolve any issues identified.

Service Strategy looks at the three types of Service Provider:

- Internal service provider
- Shared service unit
- External service provider

This is a simplified view of reality for many organisations but is a useful way of differentiating the types. Each type of service provider has its own characteristics and is applicable to different situations. The commercial nature of the provider is usually the driver for the decision on which type is appropriate.

The IT Service Provider's approach to Service Strategy is examined and highlighted by the four Ps of Strategy:

- Strategy as a **Perspective**. This includes the IT Service Provider's vision, direction and philosophy of how to do business.
- Strategy as a **Position**. This centres on the IT Service Provider's approach to making Services available, for example low cost or maximum added value.
- Strategy as a **Plan**. This incorporates a route map to move the IT Service Provider as an organisation from where they are now to where they want to be.
- Service Strategy as a **Pattern**. This is a consistent and repeatable method of making strategic decisions.

The Processes of Service Strategy are:

- IT Financial Management
- Demand Management
- Service Portfolio Management
- Strategy Generation

SERVICE DESIGN

Service Design takes the strategy developed within the Service Strategy part of the Lifecycle as the starting point for developing new services (and improving existing services). These new services (and improvements to existing services) are introduced to the live environment through Service Transition.

Service Design's objective is to create cost-effective services that provide the level of quality required to meet the demands of customers and stakeholders. Good Service Design allows faster and simpler introduction of new services (or improvements to existing services) as well as providing better governance, ensuring compliance to legal requirements and corporate rules. Lower cost services are another advantage of Service Design as support and improvement costs are controlled and lowered. Service Design also ensures the services provide the required levels of quality as well as mapping to business and customer needs. The ability to measure the quality of services better is another advantage that supports decision making and leads to continual improvement.

There are five major aspects of Service Design:

- The introduction of new or changed services. Business requirements are identified, distilled, negotiated and agreed.
- The Service Management systems and tools. These include the Service Catalogue and the Service Portfolio.
- The capability of technology architectures and management systems to operate and maintain new services (and improvements to existing services).
- The capability of all Service Management processes to operate and maintain new services (and improvements to existing services).
- The design of measurement methods and metrics. Measurement methods and metrics are needed to analyse the performance of services. This supports decision making and leads to continual improvement.

The Processes of Service Design are:

- Service Catalogue Management
- Service Level Management
- Supplier Management
- Capacity Management
- Availability Management
- IT Service Continuity Management
- Information Security Management

SERVICE TRANSITION

Service Transition takes the output from Service Design and then implements it into the live environment ensuring that disruption and impact on other live services is understood and eradicated or at least minimised. Service Transition acts as the bridge between Service Design and Service Operation and operates in an area that historically has caused tensions in organisations, that is the transition from development into live. Successful and well-managed Service Transition will remove any risk of the 'thrown over the wall accusation' often heard from Service Operation areas following the introduction of a new service (or change to an existing service).

Service Transition aims to set and manage customer expectations around new or improved services as well as reducing the introduction of known errors and reducing the variations between predicted and actual performance. Implementation without disruption is important to business areas and this is what Service Transition strives for, while also ensuring that the new service does what it is supposed to do.

The degree to which user, customer and Service Management staff satisfaction and confidence can be boosted by successful implementation is substantial. Unfortunately, the opposite is also true with poor implementations having an adverse impact on satisfaction, confidence and morale.

Service Transition is involved with the planning and management of the resources required to introduce and activate new or improved services. This needs to be done within agreed cost, risk and time parameters. Communication is a crucial part of Service Transition and effective communication will reduce the risk of adverse impact and unsuccessful implementations.

The Processes of Service Transition are:

- Knowledge Management
- Service Asset and Configuration Management
- Change Management
- Release and Deployment Management
- Transition Planning and Support
- Service Validation and Testing
- Evaluation

SERVICE OPERATION

Service Operation is the phase of the IT Service Management Lifecycle that is responsible for 'business as usual' activities. If services are not properly utilised or are not delivered efficiently and effectively, they will not deliver their full value, regardless of how well designed they might be. It is Service Operation that is responsible for using and channelling the processes to deliver services to users and customers.

Service Operation is where the value that has been modelled in Service Strategy and confirmed through Service Design and Service Transition is actually delivered.

Without Service Operation running the services as designed and using the processes as designed, there would be no control and management of the services. Production of meaningful metrics by Service Operation will form the basis and starting point for service improvement activity.

The purpose of Service Operation is to organise and conduct the activities and processes needed to deliver services to business users at agreed levels of service. Service Operation is also responsible for the ongoing management of the infrastructure and applications technology that is used to support and deliver the services. This infrastructure and applications technology underpins the support and delivery of the services.

Service Operation is a balancing act. It is not just a matter of carrying out the processes on a day-to-day basis. There is a dynamic 'debate' that is always taking place on four levels. These are known as the Four Balances of Service Operation:

- **Internal IT view versus external business view:** The external business view will relate to the services delivered to users and customers while, internally within IT, those services will be viewed as a number of components.

- **Stability versus responsiveness:** Changes are frequently the cause of Incidents and loss of availability, so it may be tempting to limit the number of changes in order to boost the stability of services. However, changes will always be needed in order to keep service up to date and to adapt to evolving business needs. The balance is being able to respond speedily to changes while still focusing on the stability of the infrastructure.

- **Quality of service versus cost of service:** There will always be pressures to boost the quality of IT services while controlling costs. Intense budgetary pressures may lead to reduced levels of service with more failures and less support. The key is to have a meaningful dialogue over costs ensuring that the business fully understands what it gets and does not get for a certain amount of money and what it would get if it spent a bit less or a bit more.

- **Reactive versus proactive:** An extremely proactive organisation will always be predicting where things could go wrong and taking action to mitigate or prevent the situation. Taken to the extreme, such organisations may over monitor and apply unnecessary changes. Conversely, organisations that are purely reactive spend most of their time 'fire fighting' and dealing with situations as they arise, and they need to move more to the 'fire prevention' approach of predicting and avoiding Incidents and Problems.

The Processes of Service Operation are:

- Access Management
- Request Fulfilment
- Incident Management
- Problem Management
- Event Management

The Functions of Service Operation are:

- The Service Desk
- IT Operations Management
- Application Management
- Technical Management

CONTINUAL SERVICE IMPROVEMENT

Continual Service Improvement is an important phase of the Service Lifecycle because it ensures that Service Management implementations continue to deliver the desired business benefits. Continual Service Improvement is responsible for ensuring that improvements are identified and implemented. One of the main objectives of Continual Service Improvement is to improve the cost-effectiveness of delivering IT services without adversely impacting customer satisfaction. The performance of the IT Service Provider is always being measured and improvements are made to processes, IT services and the IT infrastructure in order to boost efficiency, effectiveness and cost-effectiveness.

RELATED MATERIAL

The material that makes up the ITIL core tends to remain fairly constant while the Complementary material is more subject to change and development. Complementary material may be in the form of publications and web-based material from the wider industry. Market sector-specific material is produced as well as vendor publications.

ITIL is complementary to the ISO/IEC 20000 standard. Additionally, it can work in hand with a number of other standards, frameworks and approaches. None of these in isolation will provide an organisation with everything it needs; the key is to adapt and adopt those parts of the guidelines that are relevant in order to develop a systematic approach. These complementary approaches include:

- **COBIT:** Control Objectives for Information and related Technology provides best practice and guidance for the management of IT processes.
- **EFQM:** The European Foundation for Quality Management is a framework for organisational management systems.
- **CMMI-SVC:** Capability Maturity Model Integration is a process improvement approach that allows organisations to benchmark themselves against other organisations operating in similar spheres. CMMI-SVC is specifically aimed at service establishment, service management and service delivery.
- **PRINCE2®:** The methodology for project management produced by the UK government.

"PRINCE2® is a Registered Trade Mark of the Office of Government Commerce in the United Kingdom and other countries"

- **Balanced Scorecard:** Strategy is disseminated into certain Key Performance Indicators (KPIs) that can then be reported on.
- **ISO/IEC 19770:** Software Asset Management standard.
- **ISO/IEC 27001:** Information Security Management specification.
- **Six Sigma:** A business management strategy.
- **eSCM-SP:** eSourcing Capability Model for Service Providers.
- **SOX:** The Sarbannes-Oxley framework for corporate governance.

2 THE CONCEPT OF SERVICE, ITS VALUE PROPOSITION AND COMPOSITION

Main book references: SS 2.2, SD 2.2

Services deliver value to customers. Value is created by providing the right Service under the right conditions. A service is a means of delivering value to customers by facilitating outcomes that customers want to achieve without the ownership of specific costs and risks.

Customers or business areas will want outcomes but will not want the associated costs and risks of ownership. For example, a self-service till within a supermarket will require network connectivity to allow sales to be recorded and stock to be reordered. The business area responsible for the till will not want all the costs, risks and management issues of maintaining the network. They are content to take this as a Service from a Service Provider (which could be internal, external or a shared service unit). Such a Service Provider will have the necessary network knowledge and skills to deliver the Service. These are not skills that the business area wants to obtain and maintain. The business area agrees to pay for the network service subject to specific terms and conditions. In this way Resources are utilised effectively. If individual business areas were all responsible for their networks, there would be considerable waste through duplication and any number of other issues including lack of compatibility, lack of investment, lack of up-to-date knowledge, inability to leverage economies of scale etc.

From the viewpoint of the customer, value is made up of two elements. These are Utility (or fitness for purpose) and Warranty (or fitness for use).

UTILITY

Utility is the functionality offered by a product or service to meet a particular need. Utility is often summarised as 'what it does'.

Utility is value in the sense of what the customer gets from the Service. This may be by allowing or facilitating tasks to be performed better in relation to the outcome desired by the business area or by reducing or removing constraints on the business area's ability to achieve their desired outcomes.

Utility centres on what the Service actually does, which determines whether it is fit for purpose.

WARRANTY

Warranty is a promise or guarantee that a product or service will meet its agreed requirements.

Warranty is value in the sense of how the Utility is delivered to the customer. The determination of whether a Service is fit for use (i.e. the positive effect of the Service being available when and where it is required) takes into account whether there is sufficient capacity and whether the Service is dependable in terms of security and continuity for it to be relied on.

Utility and Warranty have to be viewed together in that neither of them can deliver full value on their own. Figure 2.1 illustrates that value is only created when both Utility and Warranty are satisfied.

Figure 2.1 Logic of value creation through Services (Source: OGC ITIL Service Strategy ISBN 978-0-113310-45-6)

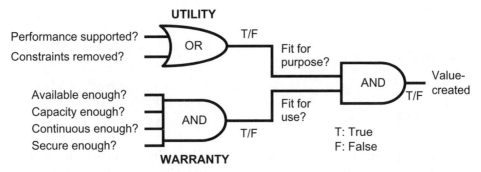

It may be that a Service does exactly what the customer or business area wants (Utility), but if the Service is unreliable or lacks the necessary security or availability levels (Warranty), then it cannot deliver maximum value. Conversely, a high availability, highly secure and highly reliable Service that does not actually do what the customer or business area requires will again not deliver maximum value. Customers or business areas can only derive maximum value from a Service if both Utility and Warranty are satisfied.

A Value chain is a way of viewing a series of activities or processes all of which add value. By breaking it down to its component parts, it is easier to identify areas for improvement.

VALUE CHAIN

A Value Chain is a sequence of processes that creates a product or service that is of value to a customer. Each step of the sequence builds on the previous steps and contributes to the overall product or service.

However, Service Management is really more about a group of interlocking processes and closely communicating areas with exchanges between them rather than a series of activities. These interlocking processes and closely communicating areas can be viewed as a Value Network. Value Networks may not be (and often are not) completely internal to organisations.

VALUE NETWORK

A Value Network is a web of relationships that generates tangible and intangible value through complex dynamic exchanges through two or more organisations. Value is generated through the exchange of knowledge, information, goods or services.

Service Providers create value by using their assets (service assets) in the form of resources and capabilities.

RESOURCE

A generic term that includes IT infrastructure, people, money or anything else that might help to deliver an IT Service. Resources are considered to be assets of an organisation.

The main difference between resource assets and capability assets is that usually resources can be purchased from the market, but capabilities have to be developed over time. Therefore, it tends to be easier to obtain resources than to obtain capabilities.

CAPABILITIES

The abilities of an organisation, person, Process, application, Configuration Item or IT Service to carry out an Activity. Capabilities are intangible assets of an organisation.

Capabilities are important because they tend to be in the DNA of an organisation and are often intangible. They are built up over a period of time and provide a differentiator for a particular organisation that can then be turned into a competitive advantage. Capabilities reflect the knowledge, experience and culture of an organisation, and are used to transform physical resources into services.

Figure 2.2 shows how an IT Service Provider creates services by using service assets in the form of resources and capabilities.

___

Figure 2.2 Service delivery through service assets (Source: OGC ITIL Service Strategy ISBN 978-0-113310-45-6)

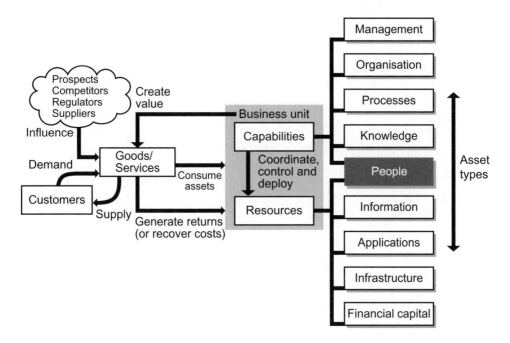

A Service Model describes how a Service Provider is able to generate value for a particular group of customer contracts by connecting together (and generating interaction between) the customer's assets and the Service Provider's assets. The interaction means that demand is connected to the capacity or ability to serve. A Service Model describes both the structure and the dynamics of the service:

- **Structure:** How service assets are needed and the patterns in which they are needed in order to deliver service.
- **Dynamics:** These are interactions between the Service Provider and the customer or business area and include the activities and the flow of activities. Patterns of Business Activity (PBA), demand patterns, variations and exceptions all make up the dynamics of a service.

The structure and dynamics are influenced by the make-up and balance of Utility and Warranty to be delivered to customers or business areas.

A Service Model may include:

- Process Maps
- Workflow Diagrams
- Activity Patterns
- Queuing Models

Once a Service Model is in place, variants can be created that can be used to create a bespoke service applicable to a particular customer's requirements.

3 THE FUNCTIONS AND PROCESSES ACROSS THE LIFECYCLE

Main book references: SS 2.6, ST 2.3

The terms 'Function' and 'Process' are important within ITIL. ITIL contains Processes or sets of Activities to achieve specific Objectives, for example the Objective of Incident Management is to restore Service with the minimum of adverse impact as quickly as possible. The individuals who carry out this Process are part of a team (i.e. the Service Desk). The Service Desk is a Function.

PROCESS

A Process is a structured set of Activities designed to accomplish a specific Objective. A Process takes one or more defined inputs and turns them into defined outputs. A Process may include any of the roles, responsibilities, tools and management controls required to deliver the outputs reliably. A Process may define policies, standards, guidelines, activities and work instructions if they are needed.

FUNCTION

A Function is a team or group of people and the tools they use to carry out one or more Processes or Activities (e.g. the Service Desk).

A Function is a structural part or unit of an organisation. Functions are set up to carry out particular types of work and to be responsible for certain specific outcomes. They have service assets in order to enable them to achieve their designated outcomes. These service assets take the form of Resources and Capabilities. Resources are allocated to Functions, and Capabilities are built up over time.

Functions are specialised and have their own skills and knowledge base. They carry out Activities that are parts of Processes. They may carry out a whole Process, but often will share Processes with other Functions. Where this happens, it is important that responsibilities are clear and that good communication channels are in place. Coordination between Functions is a key part of organisational design.

Historically, organisations have often operated with functions isolated from each other. This is not surprising given the specialised and sometimes narrow nature of what they do. The use of processes and process models is important in ensuring that functions work together and communicate properly.

Individuals within a function have a defined role. These roles are carried out in order to achieve the desired outcomes.

ROLE

A set of responsibilities, activities and authorities granted to a person or team. A Role is defined in a Process. One person or team may have multiple Roles (e.g. the Roles of Configuration Manager and Change Manager may be carried out by a single person).

A role is a description of what an individual actually does. All organisations define the roles needed to carry out the required tasks and individuals are allocated to these roles.

When considering roles, it is important to remember that a role can be undertaken by more than one person and that a person can undertake more than one role.

There are two key generic roles that are important:

- **Process Owner:** The Process Owner is accountable for making sure that all parts of a process are carried out. The Process owner is responsible for:

  o defining the strategy of the process

  o helping with the design of the process

  o drawing up and communicating policies and standards to be followed by those operating the process

  o ensuring that the process is being followed in line with its design at all times

  o always looking for possible process improvements and feeding these into the Service Improvement Plan

  o examining any suggested enhancements and feeding these into the Service Improvement Plan as appropriate

  o ensuring that all staff carrying out the process have had the correct training in order to operate the process

  o auditing the process to ensure effectiveness and efficiency

  o setting up and monitoring Key Performance Indicators.

- **Service Owner:** The Service Owner is accountable for a specific service. The Service Owner is responsible for:

  o being available to customers as the primary point of contact within the IT Service Provider in relation to the service

  o being available to customers in order to deal with queries and issues around the service

  o ensuring that the service is delivered in accordance with its Service Level Agreement (SLA)

  o making sure that the service is effectively monitored

  o acting as the escalation point in relation to major incidents impacting the service

  o representing the service in meetings with customers

  o representing the service and working alongside Supplier Management in meetings with suppliers

  o representing the service within the IT Service Provider including attendance as appropriate at the Change Advisory Board

  o taking part in negotiating Service Level Agreements (SLAs) and Operational Level Agreements (OLAs) in relation to the service

  o making sure that the service is accurately represented and that all information in relation to the service is up to date within the Service Catalogue

  o constantly looking for possible service improvements and feeding these into the Service Improvement Plan

  o examining any suggested enhancements and feeding these into the Service Improvement Plan as appropriate.

Organisations will often produce an Authority Matrix in order to set out clearly the specific roles and responsibilities in relation to Processes. One of the best known examples of an Authority Matrix is the RACI model. RACI is an acronym representing Responsible, Accountable, Consulted and Informed. Each of these is a manner in which a role can be involved in a Process. Organisations use RACI in order to map the process activities to the roles that undertake these activities.

Responsible	undertakes the process or activity	(undertakes the work)
Accountable	is the owner of the output and of the quality of that output	(owner)
Consulted	provides input from knowledge and experience	(provides assistance)
Informed	receives information about the process activity	(needs to know)

There must be one accountable role for each activity. Each activity must have a role that is Responsible and each activity must have a role that is Accountable. The Consulted and Informed are optional and their inclusion will depend on the nature of the process. It is key that the roles and activities are allocated to specified individuals within the organisation. It is important to understand that roles and processes can be undertaken by a number of individuals within an organisation but there will only be one ultimate owner. For example, the Problem Manager will be accountable for the resolution of problems within an organisation. However, Problem Management will take place in a large number of areas across the organisation. The individuals undertaking Problem Management will often be in separate teams in different parts of the organisational design or structure of the organisation but conduct a process as part of a 'virtual' team.

Separating the role from the organisational structure has a number of advantages:

- It allows the same process or activity to be undertaken by more than one role or team.
- It enables the process model to remain undisturbed when organisational design changes occur.
- It allows organisations that have multiple sites, often in multiple countries, to aggregate responsibilities in fewer roles in smaller sites.
- It allows the same underpinning process model to be used regardless of the complexity and diversity of the business being supported. The complexity and diversity are represented in the organisational design and structure rather than in the process model.

Processes are made up of a set of coordinated activities using resources and capabilities to arrive at an outcome. These activities create value (directly or indirectly) for a customer.

The Process structure diagram (Figure 3.1) shows how a Process is made up of a number of elements. A Process receives inputs and transforms them into defined outputs by using various enablers. These enablers are the Capabilities and Resources. The outputs are produced in a 'closed loop' that allows for feedback and then improvement. The Process control elements are there to ensure that the Process is consistent and repeatable. Process control also ensures that the Process is managed effectively and efficiently.

A Process is initiated by a trigger or an Event. It then transforms inputs into outputs via a series of Activities undertaken by systems or people. These Activities have documented work instructions or procedures while the people involved have designated roles. Every Process has an owner responsible for it. The Process control element in Figure 3.1 gives the governance and control required to ensure that the Process does what it is supposed to do. This is also helped by the existence of documented Objectives, policy and terms of reference. Metrics allow the Process to be measured in terms of cost and quality and allow for feedback into the 'loop'.

Figure 3.1 The generic process elements (Source: OGC ITIL Service Design ISBN 978-0-113310-47-0)

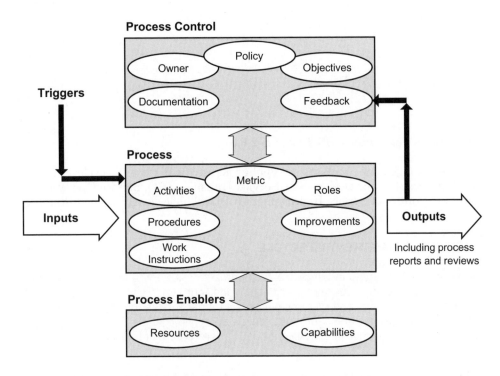

All Processes have certain characteristics:

- **Responds to a specific trigger:** All Processes have a specific trigger. It does not matter whether a Process is continual or whether it builds over time, there will always be a specific trigger.

- **Specific results:** The Process is there to produce a designated result that needs to be identifiable.

- **Customers:** Each Process delivers output(s) to a customer who will have expectations that need to be met. Customers may be internal or external to the organisation.

- **Measurable:** Processes need to be able to be measured in terms of cost and quality. The robust measurement of Process performance is the starting point for Process improvement Activities.

4 THE ROLE OF PROCESSES IN THE SERVICE LIFECYCLE

Main book references: SS 2.6.2, SS 2.6.3

Service Management Processes are applied across the Service Lifecycle. Service Strategy (SS), Service Design (SD), Service Transition (ST), Service Operation (SO) and Continual Service Improvement (CSI) all have clearly defined Processes.

SERVICE MANAGEMENT LIFECYCLE

The Service Management Lifecycle is an approach to IT Service Management that emphasises the importance of coordination and control across the various Functions, Processes and systems necessary to manage the full lifecycle of IT Services. The Service Management Lifecycle approach considers the strategy, design, transition, operation and continuous improvement of IT Services.

A lifecycle is a representation of the various stages a service or component goes through. It also applies to Incidents, Problems and Changes. The lifecycle approach is a powerful way of viewing a Service.

LIFECYCLE

The lifecycle represents various stages in the life of an IT Service, Configuration Item, Incident, Problem, Change etc. The lifecycle defines the categories for status and the status transitions that are permitted. For example:

- The lifecycle of an application includes requirements, design, build, deploy, operate, optimise.
- The expanded Incident lifecycle includes detect, respond, diagnose, repair, recover, restore.
- The lifecycle of a server may include ordered, received, in test, live, disposed etc.

The Service Lifecycle is initiated from a change in business requirements. Once identified, these new or changed requirements are agreed and documented at the Service Strategy stage of the Lifecycle. They are documented as packages, each with a specified set of business outcomes. Service Design takes the package from Service Strategy and produces a service solution. This service solution defines and sets out all that will be needed to take the service or service improvement all the way through the rest of the Service Lifecycle. The solution(s) may be internally developed, bought in and configured internally or a combination of the two.

The output from Service Design is a design definition that is passed to the Service Transition phase of the Lifecycle. Here the service or service improvement is built, evaluated, tested and the testing validated prior to being transitioned into the live environment. Once in the live environment it is in the Service Operation phase, although Service Transition will still be involved in Early Life Support (ELS). Service Operation is where the value is actually delivered and measured because operational services are provided to produce the required business outcomes.

Opportunities for improvement may be identified at any stage in the Lifecycle. Continual Service Improvement uses the efficiency, effectiveness and cost-effectiveness measurement and reporting to highlight areas for improvement. These measurements and reporting are generated in the Service Operation phase; however, improvement may be identified as required in any of the earlier stages.

A lifecycle approach demands specialisation and coordination that are facilitated by feedback and control. Figure 4.1 illustrates the logical flow through Strategy, Design, Transition, Operation and Continual Improvement but also shows the feedback and control points.

Figure 4.1 Service Management Processes are applied across the Service Lifecycle
(Source: OGC ITIL Service Strategy ISBN 978-0-113310-45-6)

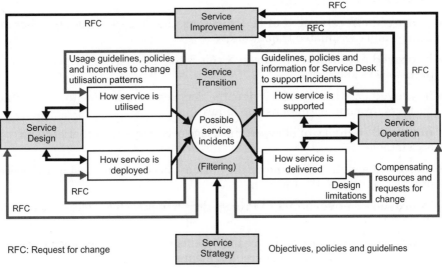

There is an interrelationship between Functions, Processes and Roles throughout the Service Lifecycle. Processes can cut across one or more Functions and necessitate Activities to be carried out by one or more Roles within any Function.

5 HOW SERVICE MANAGEMENT CREATES BUSINESS VALUE

Main book references: SS 3.1, ST 2.4.3, SD 2.4.3, SO 2.4.3, CSI 3.7.2

There are a number of ways in which Service Management creates business value. Each stage of the Service Lifecycle provides value to the business. It is through Service Operation where the value is actually seen. This value, observed in Service Operation, would have been modelled in Service Strategy. Service Design and Transition would have designed, tested and validated the Cost of the Service, while Continual Service Improvement would have identified measures and methods for optimising the performance of the Service.

Service Management creates business value through:

- **improved quality of service:** quality is designed into Services and this follows through the rest of the Service Lifecycle;

- **improved consistency of service:** consistent repeatable Processes generate consistent Services;

- **improved effectiveness of IT Processes:** the Processes work together in a defined and coordinated framework;

- **improved availability of service:** this is the most obvious aspect of Service to customers and users;

- **improved continuity of service:** the Services will continue to support the business through disruptions and failures;

- **improved security of service:** the usage of Services is authorised and accountable;

- **improved service alignment:** the business needs are not lost as a Service progresses through the Lifecycle

- **improved IT governance:** a Process-driven approach enables controls to be instigated;

- **improved information:** the measurements and metrics designed in Service Design in response to business requirements and delivered in Service Operation provide information and triggers for Continual Service Improvement;

- **improved decision making:** the availability of improved information enables decisions to be made in the light of actual performance;

- **more effective service performance:** quality and cost-effectiveness are designed into the Processes – Financial, Capacity, Continuity and Availability are all taken into account;

- **reduced total cost of ownership (TCO):** costs are understood and controlled throughout the Lifecycle;

- **easier implementation of new services or changed services:** an integrated approach with clear Processes, Roles and responsibilities.

6 HOW SERVICE OFFERINGS AND AGREEMENTS SUPPORT THE SERVICE LIFECYCLE

Main book references: SS 5.1 up to 5.1.2, 5.3 up to 5.3.1, 5.5.1, SD 2.4.5

The Service Offerings and Agreements Processes all support the Service Lifecycle. The value added by them cannot really be viewed in isolation because the real value will only be generated as they interface with other Processes through the Lifecycle.

- **Service Portfolio Management:** This ensures that the maximum value is delivered to an organisation once an investment decision has been taken. Service Portfolio Management ensures that there is an effective method for evaluating investments in place and then makes sure the investments are managed effectively throughout their lifecycles. This includes ensuring proper governance arrangements are put in place and that the investments and the original business cases are assessed on an ongoing basis to take into account changing circumstances and to make sure benefits are realised.

- **Service Catalogue Management:** This produces and maintains the Service Catalogue and ensures that it contains up-to-date and accurate information on all services (those in operation and those being prepared for operation). It ensures that the Service Catalogue is in place and that it meets the requirements of all those who need to use it in terms of availability, accessibility and performance.

- **Service Level Management:** This supports the Service Lifecycle by ensuring that all services have negotiated, agreed and documented Service Level Agreements in place and that monitoring and reporting procedures are in place to make sure that the agreed level of service is being delivered. It builds and maintains effective relationships with customers and business areas. Services are managed to ensure that agreed levels of performance are delivered and systems are put in place to make sure that service levels can be continually improved (if appropriate and cost justified).

- **Demand Management:** This understands and influences customer demand for services. This is done in order to support the delivery and management of minimum capacity to meet these demands. It aims to avoid uncertainty in demand. Such uncertainty in demand would lead to the risk of either service degradation or excess capacity being put in place. By moving workload to less busy times, the use of capacity is optimised and more efficient use is made of resources. More efficient use of resources occurs because utilisation is evened out, with the need to cater for peaks and troughs reduced.

- **Supplier Management:** This ensures that suppliers are managed and that the services they supply are also managed so value is obtained. It also ensures that the service delivered to the business areas is transparent in the sense that it does not matter in terms of the quality of the service that some or all of the service has been provided by a third party. Supplier Management contributes to the Service Lifecycle by ensuring that the organisation gets the best value from the supplier throughout the lifecycle of the relationship. Supplier Management builds and maintains effective and constructive relationships with suppliers. Good management of the Supplier and Contract Database helps in this respect.

- **Financial Management:** This supports the Service Lifecycle by raising the visibility of costs at all stages and ensuring that the financial resources available are fully aligned to the organisation's plans and the business demand for IT Services. This is done through robust and effective financial planning and budgeting as well as by making sure that all financial expenditure is accounted for. The costs of all IT Services, activities and processes are measured allowing action to be taken if necessary.

Table 6.1 details the ITIL V3 Service Management Process and Functions indicating which core book they are covered in or section of the Lifecycle they fall under. Most of the Processes play a part during each phase of the Service Management Lifecycle. The shaded Processes are covered in detail in this book.

Table 6.1 Location of Processes and Functions within the Lifecycle stages

Function or process	Core book/Phase of lifecycle
Demand management	Service Strategy
Financial management	Service Strategy
Service portfolio management	Service Strategy
Strategy generation	Service Strategy
Availability management	Service Design
Capacity management	Service Design
Information security management	Service Design
IT service continuity management	Service Design
Service catalogue management	Service Design
Service level management	Service Design
Supplier management	Service Design
Change management	Service Transition

(Continued)

Table 6.1 *(Continued)*

Function or process	Core book / Phase of lifecycle
Evaluation	Service Transition
Knowledge management	Service Transition
Management of organisational and stakeholder change	Service Transition
Release and deployment management	Service Transition
Service asset and configuration management	Service Transition
Service validation and testing	Service Transition
Transition planning and support	Service Transition
Access management	Service Operation
Application management (function)	Service Operation
Event management	Service Operation
Incident management	Service Operation
IT operations (function)	Service Operation
Problem management	Service Operation
Request fulfilment	Service Operation
Service desk (function)	Service Operation
Technical management (function)	Service Operation
Service measurement	Continual Service Improvement
Service reporting	Continual Service Improvement
Seven-step improvement process	Continual Service Improvement

SECTION 2:
THE SOA PROCESSES AND
FUNCTIONS

7   SERVICE PORTFOLIO MANAGEMENT

INTRODUCTION

The Service Portfolio Management process is an important part of Service Strategy and Service Offerings and Agreements. It is the process that gives a holistic view at a management level of all of an organisation's services as they move through the Service Lifecycle.

There are three key constituent parts that make up the Service Portfolio: the Service Pipeline, the Service Catalogue and Retired Services.

The Service Pipeline
The Service Pipeline contains information on services that are under development. These are the future services for an organisation and they will (in due course, following design, development and testing) be transitioned into the live environment. The organisation's future growth plans and strategic approach are reflected by the contents of the pipeline.

Examining the contents of the Service Pipeline at any particular point in time provides a snapshot of an organisation's future plans and also gives an indication of the health of the organisation in the sense of indicating the level of strategic activity taking place. The use of the term 'pipeline' might suggest that all services move at speed through it. This is not necessarily the case. Some services may be fast-tracked depending on their business criticality and other services may move through the pipeline more slowly due to the complexity of their development.

The level of an organisation's Continual Improvement activity, as well as the degree of proactive work by Service Strategy and Service Design, will be reflected in the Service pipeline volumes.

The Service Catalogue
The Service Catalogue section of the Service Portfolio sits between the Service Pipeline and Retired Services. It contains information on all services that are being delivered by Service Operation as well as all those services that are ready and approved to be transitioned into production. Importantly, the Service Catalogue is visible to customers. It is like a menu of services available to customers. The Service Catalogue represents the Service Provider's current capability whereas the Service Pipeline centres on future capability.

The Service Catalogue can be used to provide solutions for customers that are made up of more than one service. Third-party services may be included in the Service Catalogue and offered direct to customers as they are or with enhancements.

Ideally, the Service Catalogue should be integrated with the Configuration Management Database (CMDB). Such integration would allow an overall view to be taken of the outward customer facing Service Catalogue together with the internal components that make up the services. Additionally, critical areas of the infrastructure on which live services depend would be easily highlighted. Integration would allow a particular service to be viewed both from an external business perspective and from an internal technical perspective.

Retired Services

Retired Services are services that have been taken out of production and that are not in operational use. It may be that services have come to the end of their natural life, have been superseded, are no longer demanded or are no longer cost-effective. Information on those services that have been retired is stored in the organisation's Service Knowledge Management System (SKMS) because it may be useful in the future. Service Transition is responsible for the phasing out of services.

There may from time to time be demand to resurrect Retired Services. This may be possible, but care needs to be exercised because the costs may not be as before and support capabilities may have been lost or eroded.

THE SERVICE PORTFOLIO AND ITS RELATIONSHIP WITH THE SERVICE CATALOGUE AND THE SERVICE PIPELINE

Main book references: SS 4.2.3, 5.1.2.3

The Service Portfolio gives a full picture of an organisation's services. It is an overarching view of commitments and investments made by the Service Provider. Services planned and provided for all customers and in all markets are included.

Information on services under development for future delivery is held in the Service Pipeline part of the Service Portfolio while information on services in the live environment and those ready for live operation is held in the Service Catalogue part of the Service Portfolio. Information on Retired Services is also held within the Service Portfolio.

Figure 7.1 shows how the Service Pipeline, Service Catalogue and Retired Services combine to create the Service Portfolio and how they contribute to the phases of the Service Lifecycle.

The Service Catalogue is the only part of the Service Portfolio that recovers costs or makes a profit; however, financial control and governance are key parts of Service Portfolio Management. The Service Portfolio represents all the resources

Figure 7.1 Service Pipeline and Service Catalogue (Source: OGC ITIL Service Strategy ISBN 978-0-113310-45-6)

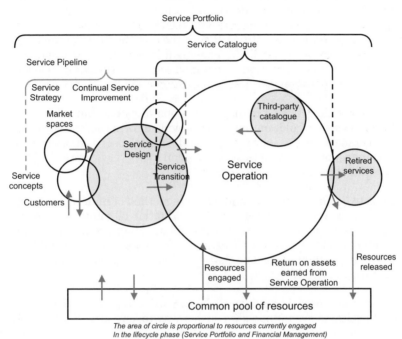

The area of circle is proportional to resources currently engaged
In the lifecycle phase (Service Portfolio and Financial Management)

across the phases of the Service Lifecycle. Each phase of the Lifecycle will need resources to complete tasks bringing funding requirements. It is important that movements between phases have agreed funding in place together with a plan for recovering costs.

The Service Portfolio provides the basis for managing all services through the full Service Lifecycle in terms of their:

- business requirements;
- business case for investment;
- value proposition;
- funding and other resources for development;
- funding and other resources for transition;
- funding and other resources for operation;
- funding and other resources for continual improvement;
- risks associated with development, transition and operation;
- pricing.

The goal of Service Portfolio Management is to make sure that all decisions to invest in IT services are based on sound principles and that the investment decisions are in line with the business priorities and requirements. When an investment decision has been made, the investment is then managed through the various phases of the Service Lifecycle with Service Portfolio Management making sure that value generation is optimised with the costs being controlled and the benefits realised. Service Portfolio Management is the area of an organisation that is able to provide information on planned services, services in development, services ready for operation, services in operation and retired services.

The Service Portfolio acts as a managerial support system that allows the organisation to gather, hold, manage and provide information on services as well as on the customers for the services and on the risks, costs and pricing. Service Portfolio Management enables the organisation to set service priorities and to allocate resources in line with those priorities.

There needs to be an understood and effective method of making investment decisions based on a standard approach to the evaluation of potential investments in IT Services. It is an objective of Service Portfolio Management to ensure that this standard approach to evaluating investment decisions is in place and that it is followed. The investment decisions that have been made are then managed throughout the Service Lifecycle.

A governance framework should be in place in order to make sure that the agreed investment decisions are managed in such a way through the Service Lifecycle so that the benefits originally realised are delivered. There also needs to be ongoing reassessment of each investment decision and its benefits in the light of changing conditions and circumstances. Such changing conditions and circumstances will be both internal to the organisation and external in the wider environment. External changes may involve customers, suppliers, competitors, technological advances and changes in legislation.

Service Portfolio Management has a number of objectives:

- To develop, populate and maintain a Service Portfolio that is able to give a holistic view of all services and to indicate the status of all services where status includes planned, in development, ready for operation, in operation and retired.

- To put in place a set of criteria that new services have to meet in order to be included in the Service Portfolio. This may take the form of a 'route map' that those proposing investments in IT Services have to follow in order to meet the necessary requirements and conditions to allow admission to the Service Portfolio.

- To ensure that the Service Portfolio has the functionality and scope to meet the requirements of users.

- To ensure that the Service Portfolio delivers the performance, availability and security required by users.

- To ensure that a Service Pipeline is developed and managed as an integral part of the Service Portfolio.

- To ensure that a Service Catalogue is developed and managed as an integral part of the Service Portfolio.

- To ensure that a store for information on retired services is developed and managed as an integral part of the Service Portfolio. Such a store is part of the Service Knowledge Management System.

- To put in place the governance framework to cover the triggers and controls for moving services from the Service Pipeline to the Service Catalogue and from the Service Catalogue to the store for Retired Services.

- To ensure that reporting requirements are agreed and that reports and metrics are produced and distributed in a timely fashion.

The Service Catalogue is the visible element of the Service Portfolio made available to customers. Customers will tend to be more interested in what the Service Provider can provide now rather than what might be provided in the future. That said, future service information from the Service Pipeline may also be useful if a customer is looking for a solution that is not currently available. Likewise, there will be times when information on Retired Services will be useful to customers looking for a particular solution.

Organisations with a number of customers or organisations that operate in more than one market may have more than one Service Catalogue. Where this is the case, each Service Catalogue is a reflection of the organisation's operational capability in respect of that customer or market. Each Service Catalogue is a presentation from the Service Portfolio. There are obviously very strong links between Service Portfolio Management and Service Catalogue Management.

Financial Management also plays a strong role in influencing the activities of Service Portfolio Management. If all the costs that make up a service are fully understood, comparisons can then be made with other Service Providers in order to benchmark. It may be that services can be brought in from third parties at a lower cost than they can be sourced in-house. This may be due to the economies of scale enjoyed by the third-party supplier.

Organisations are keen to concentrate on their core business and to harness their resources and capabilities in these areas. Where a service is outside their core business or where it can be sourced from outside at a lower cost than it can be produced inside, then third-party sourcing will be used. It is not in an organisation's best interests to retain and tie up resources and capabilities in areas where the service can be brought and bought in at a lower cost. However, there will be occasions where services will be produced in-house despite there being cheaper outsourced alternatives due to security considerations or the business critical need for continuity of service.

The services within the Service Catalogue are subdivided or grouped into Lines of Business in order to bring similar and complementary services together and to enable customers to more easily identify what fits with the demand that they have. Therefore the Lines of Business groupings are matched with Patterns of Business Activity (see Chapter 10 – Demand Management) that they can support. It becomes easier to identify which areas are performing better than others by adopting Lines of Business groupings within the Service Catalogue, and this enables resources to be allocated in line with the more successful and growing services and markets.

One grouping often seen within a Service Catalogue is Third-party Services. These services may be offered in the form that they have been bought in or may be enhanced by the Service Provider. A useful model for evaluating potential third-party suppliers and their services is provided by the eSourcing Capability Model for Service Providers (eSCM-SP) developed by Carnegie Mellon University. Sometimes third-party services are used if present capability does not match demand and, as such, they are used in the interim until new services can progress through the Service Pipeline to the Service Catalogue. Likewise, third-party services may be used where services have been retired as demand reduces.

Where there is a demand that cannot be met from the current Service Catalogue and where there is nothing appropriate in the Service Pipeline, there are a number of options. These range from simply not being able to provide a service, through combining with a third party to provide a service, to arranging the necessary business case evaluation to develop a service and bring it into the Service Portfolio via the Service Pipeline.

Poorly performing services may be targeted for removal from the Service Catalogue. However, this may not always be easy because they may be committed contractually for a further period or provide contingency for other services. However, it is important to monitor service performance continually from a financial perspective, taking into account the original business case together with benefits realisation to date and potential and expected future benefits realisation. Services within the Service Catalogue tie up resources and capabilities, which is why it is crucial that an organisation continually reviews the contents of its Service Catalogue and Service Portfolio.

It is important to make the best use of resources and the Service Portfolio allows an organisation to highlight where components can be standardised and reused across services. This avoids duplication of cost and effort where very similar components are required for different services. The more components that are standardised and reused, the more the organisation can realise economies of scale and reduce the cost of producing each extra unit of a component.

The Service Catalogue is the only part of the Service Portfolio that includes services in the live environment. Service Transition is involved with the movement of services into and out of the Service Catalogue. This ensures that services that are live can be fully supported. It is also important that Service Transition is involved with any changes to services within the Service Catalogue because these are services that are being relied on by customers and where there will often be a contractual obligation to deliver.

The Service Portfolio contains information on the status of all services as they move through the Service Lifecycle. The information will change as the services move from the original business case through specification of requirements, approval, design, build, test, validation, transition into live environment and eventual retirement. After being made ready for transition into the live environment the information on the service will be held in the Service Catalogue. After transition out of the live environment the information on the service will be held as Retired Services in the organisation's Service Knowledge Management System. Prior to being ready for release into the live environment, information on services will be held in the Service Pipeline.

The information held within the Service Portfolio will change and become more granular as the service evolves. Skeleton information only, including the value proposition, business case and summary details of the service, will be held in the early stages in the life of a service. However, as development gets underway, more 'meat is put on the bones' and by the time the service emerges from the Service Pipeline full information will be in place. This full information should include:

- Name of the service
- Description of the service
- Status of the service
- Owner of service – Service Provider
- Criticality of the service
- Classification of the service
- Business processes that the service underpins
- Business areas using the service
- Details of business owners
- Details of business users
- Third parties involved in delivering the service
- Applications that the service uses
- Data that the service uses
- Resources that support the service
- Details of Service Warranty Level
- Details of Service Level Requirements
- Service Level Agreement
- Underpinning Operational Level Agreements

- Underpinning third-party contracts
- Dependent services
- Supporting services
- Cost of service
- Charge for service
- Revenue for service
- Service metrics

The status of a service will include the following possibilities:

- **Service Requirements** gathered where the business area(s) have provided their initial requirements for a new or improved service or where the requirements have been gathered from within the IT Service Provider for an upgrade.
- **Service Defined**, where the requirements for the new or improved service have been assessed, defined and documented and formal Service Level Requirements issued.
- **Service Analysed**, where the requirements for the new or improved service are analysed and prioritised.
- **Service Approved**, where the Service Level Requirements have been fully completed and improved.
- **Service Chartered**, where the details of the new or improved service are communicated within the organisation and potentially to customers, and where the necessary funding has been put in place.
- **Service Designed**, where the service together with the components that make it up are designed. This may include the planned purchase of third-party components.
- **Service Developed**, where the service and the components that make it up are developed or in the case of components possibly procured.
- **Service Built**, where the new or improved service is built or put together.
- **Service Tested**, where the service is tested in isolation and in conjunction with other services that are already in operation.
- **Service Released**, where the new or improved service is released together with the components that make it up into the live environment.
- **Service Operational**, where the new service is operating in the live environment.
- **Service Retired**, where the service is no longer required.

As discussed in the previous section, when services are no longer required they are transitioned to Retired Services. A service may be retired because:

- it is no longer demanded;
- it is no longer economical to operate;
- it is no longer cost-effective;
- it has been superseded by another service.

There may be occasions where a service meets some or all of the above criteria for retirement but where the IT Service Provider wishes to retain it in the Service Catalogue. An example would be a service that acts as continuity for another critical service.

The level of information retained when a service is retired should be driven by a decision on what would be useful to keep in terms of the service being used again or in terms of information that would be useful for other potential future services.

HOW A SERVICE PORTFOLIO DESCRIBES A PROVIDER'S SERVICE AND HOW IT RELATES THE BUSINESS SERVICE WITH THE IT SERVICE

Main book reference: SS 5.3

An IT Service Provider's Service Portfolio is a strong marketing tool. The Service Portfolio represents and sets out the business needs of customers and links them to the services that are offered in response to these business needs. It is the business value described within the Service Portfolio that is important from a marketing perspective and allows comparisons to be made between services and between services offered by other service providers.

Decisions need to be made on which services to develop and offer. The IT Service Provider working closely with the business areas will identify a number of opportunities for investment in new services or investment in changing or upgrading services. Prior to any of these opportunities being turned into operational services, there has to be a decision taken on the value of the proposed service and also on its value in relation to other proposed services and existing services. The value in relation to other proposed services will determine its priority if and when a decision is taken for development to proceed and the service enters the Service Pipeline. Another area that has to be taken into consideration when reviewing potential investment decisions is whether the IT Service Provider has the capacity to develop and deliver the service and whether the marketplace has the capacity for the service.

A number of questions need to be answered from the IT Service Provider's point of view before an investment in a new or changed service can be made. These questions include:

- What value will the proposed new service or proposed changed service deliver and add to the business?

- What will be the cost of delivering the proposed new service or changed service?

- Can the cost of the proposed new service or changed service be justified and afforded?

- Why should an investment be made in this particular new service or changed service rather than in something else?

- Does the IT Service Provider have the capabilities and resources to deliver the proposed new service or changed service?

- What are the risks of developing and delivering the proposed new service or changed service?

- Is the return on investment acceptable and proportional in terms of the risks of developing and delivering the proposed new service or proposed changed service?

- Is the return on investment acceptable in terms of the investment costs of developing and delivering the proposed new service or proposed changed service?

- Is the return on investment acceptable in terms of the timescales of developing and delivering the proposed new service or proposed changed service?

- Are there any dependencies between the proposed new service or proposed changed service and other investments in the Service Pipeline?

- Are there any dependencies between the investment in the proposed new service or proposed changed service and other proposed investments in new services or changed services?

- How does the investment in the proposed new service or the proposed changed service match the overall strategy of the IT Service Provider? Is the proposed new service or proposed changed service a good fit with that strategy?

The same questions are important from an IT Service Provider's marketing standpoint, but they need to be viewed in terms of how the customer will view the proposed new service or proposed changed service. For example, two of the key questions are 'why should a customer buy this new service?' and 'why should they buy it from us?' The answers to these questions allow a marketing strategy to be developed highlighting the attributes of the new service and differentiating a particular IT Service Provider from other IT Service Providers.

The IT Service Provider will also have to consider the pricing model for the new service as well as another important strategic decision, that is how capabilities and resources should be allocated. An understanding of the IT Service Provider's strengths and weaknesses in relation to the development and delivery of a new service will also help shape the strategy.

SERVICE PORTFOLIO MANAGEMENT

A dynamic method for governing investments in Service Management across the enterprise and managing them for value.

Service Portfolio Management is a method that helps decision making around services. A Service Portfolio is much more than a mere list of current and future services. Robust Service Portfolio Management will ensure that an organisation makes investment decisions based on full information and that these investment decisions are aligned with the organisation's strategy. The absence of robust Service Portfolio Management often leads to tactical and reactive decisions that do not ultimately make strategic sense.

Service Portfolio Management should balance risk and reward for all existing and proposed services and manage changes in the Service Portfolio when conditions that influence risk and reward change over time. The Service Portfolio and Service Portfolio Management are dynamic and do not stand still.

The Service Portfolio includes information that describes the IT Service Provider's services in terms of the added value of each service and provides all the necessary information for the services to be managed throughout their lifecycle. An up-to-date and well-managed Service Portfolio, with controls and governance in place, is a powerful asset for an IT Service Provider and for an organisation.

As we have seen with marketing, there is more than one way to view a service. The service is often viewed internally within the IT Service Provider in one way, while the marketing profile couched in business terms and aimed at customers, views the service in another way. However, it is important to remember that the service remains the same regardless of the view taken.

Historically, communication and understanding between IT and business areas within organisations has not always been strong. The IT area has got on with delivering IT solutions, while the business area has concentrated on the delivery of business services. However, as both IT and the business have become more complex and more dependent on multiple capabilities and resources, there is a need for greater understanding of each other. IT Service Providers now must have a good understanding of business processes if they are going to be able to deliver IT solutions that underpin those business processes. At the same time business areas have gained an understanding of how technology can improve the effectiveness and efficiency of business processes through automation. The relationship between IT and the business has become more of a partnership within organisations.

IT Service Management brings a holistic approach to the delivery of service. It breaks down the traditional 'stovepipes' within IT and focuses more on processes across the individual IT teams. Consequently, individual IT teams, which were previously 'islands' of expertise and knowledge, are forced to communicate as part of a process. This benefits IT and the organisation as a whole. IT Service Management uses processes to focus on the capabilities and resources, and on how they come together to deliver services.

There ought to be little, if any, difference between IT services and business services in more mature organisations because they should become the same service viewed from a different perspective. The IT perspective is used to concentrate on driving further IT efficiencies and providing IT solutions while the business perspective looks at the business delivery of the IT service.

Business Service Management is the method used by the IT Service Provider to manage business services. By focusing on business services and business outcomes, it becomes easier to tie up investments and potential investments with business objectives and tangible business outcomes.

BUSINESS SERVICE MANAGEMENT

Business Service Management is the ongoing practice of governing, monitoring and reporting on IT and the business service it impacts.

Figure 7.2 shows how the value to the business increases as the IT Service Provider moves from managing at the systems or applications level, through managing at an IT services level, to managing at a Business Service level.

IT Systems Management centres on technology resources as well as infrastructure and application activity. IT Service Management focuses on IT activity while Business Service Management focuses on business activity.

Business Service Management drives the use of metrics that are focused on the business objectives. Use of such metrics allows information that is meaningful in a business sense to be derived and used to manage services and trigger continual improvement.

THE SERVICE PORTFOLIO MANAGEMENT METHODS

Main book reference: SS 5.4

Service Portfolio Management is concerned with the decision-making process that sits around whether new or improved services should be included in the Service Portfolio. This process is illustrated in Figure 7.3.

The diagram highlights the Define–Analyse–Approve–Charter loop that makes up the Service Portfolio Management Cycle. The steps of the Service Portfolio

Figure 7.2 Value to Business versus Value to IT (Source: OGC ITIL Service Strategy ISBN 978-0-113310-45-6)

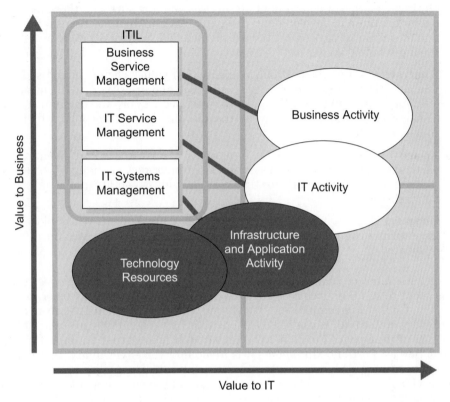

Figure 7.3 The Service Portfolio Management process (Source: OGC ITIL Service Strategy ISBN 978-0-113310-45-6)

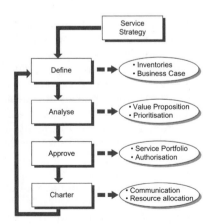

47

Management Cycle are fundamental to its operation because Service Portfolio Management is continually updating:

- **Define:** Describe and document all services, making sure that those in operation, those in development, those in predevelopment (conceptual stage) and those that have been retired are all included. Service Strategy provides the input to this stage.

- **Analyse:** Examine the portfolio to ensure that value is being maximised and that capabilities and resources are being used and prioritised in the most efficient manner in line with business objectives. Supply and demand should be balanced. The aim is to arrive at the optimum Service Portfolio, which, of course, remains dynamic.

- **Approve:** This agreement is the finalisation of the Service Portfolio at a particular point in time. Authorisation is given for new or changed services that are to be delivered and for the accompanying capability and resource requirements.

- **Charter:** This is where resources are allocated and budgets put in place and the decisions communicated within the organisation. The Service Catalogue is updated.

The environment in which the Service Portfolio operates will change over time. This needs to be taken into account. The Service Portfolio does not exist in a vacuum. Changes in competition, legislation, the costs of labour, the costs of technology etc. will all cause the decisions that have been made around the contents of the Service Portfolio to be revisited. It follows that an important role of Service Portfolio Management is to monitor the environment in order to be able to react quickly when external changes occur. The ability to have a Service Portfolio that quickly reacts to changes in the environment can give an organisation a competitive edge and reduce the risk of unexpected costs being incurred.

The following describes the Service Portfolio Management Cycle in more detail.

Define

Information needs to be gathered together. This includes information on existing services and on those services that have been retired and those that are being proposed. If an organisation produces a wish list for all the services it might want with no limit on time or capabilities or resources, this gives an indication of an unobtainable situation. However, it is a useful exercise in that it provides a view of potential scale and illuminates the debate over how best to allocate resources and capabilities. The IT Service Provider, by looking at what cannot presently be provided, is able to check the current resource and capability allocation to ensure that it remains valid when taking into account how else those scarce capabilities and resources could be allocated.

Each service within the Service Portfolio should have a business case setting out the purpose, goals and scope of the service, and how the goals and purpose are linked to, and help to deliver, the business imperatives of the organisation.

Having business case information for each service in the Service Portfolio ensures that the strategy of the organisation is visible internally and that funding decisions can be viewed in relation to other funding decisions and other funding options. This is another way of checking that the use of scarce capabilities and resources remains up to date and valid.

This part of the Service Portfolio Management Cycle occurs at the beginning of the loop and repeats as the cycle repeats. So, as well as setting out the initial set of services within the Service Portfolio, this part of the cycle revalidates the position over time. How often the Define part of the process cycle is revisited will vary from organisation to organisation and from Service Portfolio to Service Portfolio.

Different Service Portfolios will have different triggers to the Define section of the process. These triggers may be time based, for example annually or dependent on business or market circumstances. Business expansion or contraction in response to market conditions should trigger a reappraisal of the contents and validity of the current Service Portfolio. The Define stage involves the collection and checking of a large amount of information. While this collection and checking should be made as efficient as possible, the amount of effort required needs to remain proportionate to the benefits of the revalidation of the contents of the Service Portfolio at any particular point in time.

An organisation's Service Portfolio represents the strategy of that organisation. Putting a strategy into operation involves a number of decisions being made around the allocation of funds in line with the strategy priorities. The Service Portfolio Management process allows the strategy to be reflected in decisions regarding which services to develop and offer, and when they are to be developed and offered. Equally once a Service Portfolio is in place it is able to support future strategy decisions.

Decisions are required on the timing of investments and also on the order in which investments are to be made. Once made, many investment decisions are difficult to reverse both from a logistical point of view and from a cost point of view. Where a commitment has been made, it may not be possible to unravel the dependencies, which may include contractual obligations to third parties, and so plans may only be altered for future commitments.

If an investment decision is altered, the impact will be seen in the future; how far into the future will be determined by the time lag between the investment decision and deployment into the live environment. It is important to make investment decisions at the right time and in the right order. The Service Portfolio Management process provides the underpinning framework that allows this to happen. The Option Space tool (Figure 7.4) provides help to the decision-making process within Service Portfolio Management. The tool aids with decisions on the timing and order of investments.

From a Financial point of view, the Option Space tool illustrates whether the value of a service exceeds its cost. Where a service has a value-to-cost (on the x-axis) of less than one, the service is worth less than it would cost.

Figure 7.4 Option Space: focused on maintaining services (Run The Business (RTB))
(Source: OGC ITIL Service Strategy ISBN 978-0-113310-45-6)

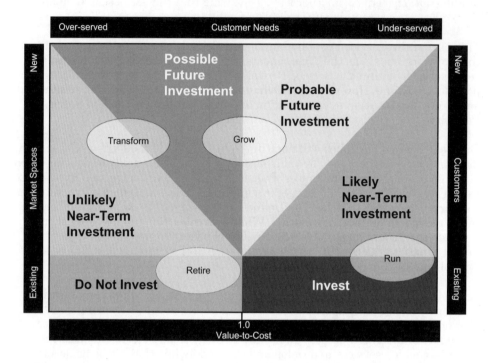

Conversely where a service has a value-to-cost of greater than one, the service has more value than it would presently cost. A value-to-cost of exactly one is neutral.

The y-axis information, such as market spaces and customers, allows the services to be viewed in terms of whether customer needs are under- or over-served in these areas. Future investment moves from being possible to probable as customer needs move from being over-served to under-served. Investment is most likely for high value-to-cost services aimed at existing customers where their needs are presently under-served.

However, value-to-cost only gives a financial perspective. There may be other factors that should be taken into consideration. These include legal and regulatory compliance, social responsibility, strategic competitiveness and other intangible factors. Therefore, the value in the value-to-cost calculation will not always be purely financial.

There are links and dependencies as with any cycle. The information needed and the effort required in the Analyse phase will have an influence on the Define phase of the Service Portfolio Management lifecycle. The Analyse phase needs to be already determined and defined in order to ensure that the correct information is gathered in the Define phase. It is important to know what data and information is going to be analysed to ensure that the correct data and information is gathered in the Define phase. Time and effort will be wasted if gathered data and information cannot be or is not intended to be analysed.

Analyse

The Analyse phase of the Service Portfolio Management process is where the strategy starts to take shape. It is suggested that the best starting point is to ask and gain answers to initially high-level questions and then 'drill' down to more detail.

Strategy is allowed to develop by asking and ascertaining what the goals of the IT Service Provider are in the long term. IT Service Providers that are internal to an organisation will also want to know the long-term goals of the organisation as a whole. For third-party commercial IT providers, the focus will be on the market's direction and competitor activity.

Having established the goals, the services needed to meet those goals can be mapped out. This allows the determination of the capabilities and resources that need to be in place in order to develop, deploy and run those services. A plan or a route map is then required to take the IT Service Provider from where it is now to where it wants to be. Such plans may cover the short, the medium and the long term.

Ascertaining the long-term goals, the services required, the capabilities and resources needed to produce these services and the plan of action gives the IT Service Provider the information required to set out what the Service Portfolio Management process needs to achieve. The analysis will develop and its focus may change as the answers to the questions are obtained and ratified. In very simple terms, the answers to 'where are we now?', 'where do we want to be?' and 'how do we get there?' greatly help the Analysis phase. The answer to 'how do we get there?' must include understanding and managing dependencies as well as risk.

The investment decisions will be based on the information that has been defined and then gathered in the Analysis phase. These investment decisions must take into account the risks of proceeding with a service and the risks of not doing so. Understanding the impact, risks and dependencies concerning investment decisions is key to balancing risk with the potential value realisation of the investment. Impact, risk, dependencies and relationships all have a part to play in the investment decisions to be made by the IT Service Provider's senior management. The ultimate value realisation of an investment decision may run across a number of business areas and may be realised in the short term, medium term or long term.

The success of the Analysis phase is closely linked and dependent on the work done during the Define phase. The success or otherwise is also dependent on gaining the involvement and input of the key stakeholders, including service experts and, most importantly, the organisation's senior management who should have the vision and budgetary discretion to drive the strategy forward. It is the senior management who will allocate the scarce resources and they need to be fully engaged and to understand the criticality of the investment decisions being made as well as the dependencies between investment decisions being taken now and those taken in the past and those likely to be taken in the future.

The strategy of the IT Service Provider will determine which type of service investments are made. There are three sorts of service investments:

- **Run the Business (RTB):** This focuses on maintaining service operations. IT Service Providers that operate as a back office cost centre would fall into this category. When viewing their Option Space Tool, in diagrammatic form, you would expect to see their investment focus on 'Run the business', with 'Grow the business' being possible in the future and 'Transform the business' being unlikely in the near term.

- **Grow the Business (GTB):** This looks to expand the organisation's range of services. When viewing their Option Space Tool, in diagrammatic form, you would expect to see their investment focus on 'Run' and 'Grow', with 'Transform' being possible in the future.

- **Transform the Business (TTB):** This centres on moving the IT Service Provider into new markets. IT Service Providers that operate as commercial providers or investment centres would fall into this category. When viewing their Option Space Tool, in diagrammatic form, you would expect to see their investment focus on 'Run', 'Grow' and 'Transform'. This is the most dynamic of the categories and is also the most likely category to retire services.

Many organisations will have different elements of each of the categories. There may be a stable core of 'Run' activity with other areas where growth and transformation are seen. The balance of allocation of funds to Run the Business, Grow the Business and Transform the Business reflects the organisation's strategy. Service Portfolio Management is the vehicle that turns the strategy into investment decisions. An organisation's dynamism and risk tolerance is also reflected in the balance between Run the Business, Grow the Business and Transform the Business investment decisions.

The three investment categories are split further into budget allocations as illustrated in Figure 7.5.

The budget allocations increase in risk as they move from Run the Business, through Grow the Business to Transform the Business. The budget allocations are:

- Core
- Non-discretionary
- Discretionary
- Growth
- Venture

Figure 7.5 Investment categories and budget allocations (Source: OGC ITIL Service Strategy ISBN 978-0-113310-45-6)

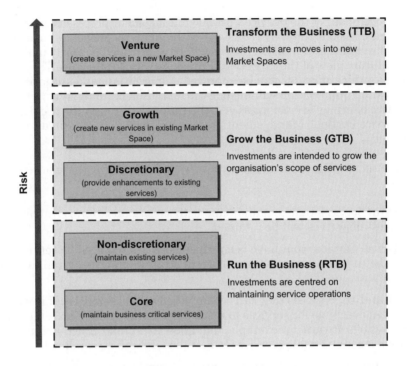

Core budget allocations have the least risk associated with them and Venture budget allocations the most. Core budget allocations centre on maintaining business critical services. Non-discretionary budget allocations are aimed at maintaining existing services while Discretionary budget allocations look to develop and deploy service enhancements for existing services. The move from Non-discretionary to Discretionary reflects the shift from Run the Business to Grow the Business.

Growth budget allocations are used to create new services within the organisation's existing markets while Venture budget allocations aim to create new services in new markets. The move from Growth to Venture reflects the shift from Grow the Business to Transform the Business.

There is another area as well as Run the Business, Grow the Business and Transform the Business where service investments are made. This revolves around retiring services. Service Portfolio Management should have clear triggers and a strategy around retiring services. It may be the case that in the short term the cost of retiring a service is in excess of the cost of running it. This may be due to one-off decommissioning costs such as contract termination or the costs of migrating the few remaining users or customers to another service. Where the short-term cost of retiring a service is in excess of the cost of running it, the budget allocation moves from being Non-discretionary to being Discretionary.

Approve

The Approve phase of the Service Portfolio Management process is where the investment decisions that have come out of the Analysis phase are ratified or otherwise. The Define and Analyse phases will have provided a clearly understood potential future view of the IT Service Provider's service offerings. These potential future service offerings will be approved if appropriate and authorised. This approval and authorisation will include the allocation of funds. Where potential new service offerings are not approved, the rationale through the previous parts of the Service Portfolio Management process will need to be revisited to see what has changed.

There are six possible results and outputs from the Approve phase for existing services:

- **Retain:** Services that remain in line with the organisation's strategy and the business objectives will be retained.

- **Replace:** Services that have been superseded are replaced by services that align better to the organisation's current strategy and the current business objectives.

- **Rationalise:** Services that can be simplified are rationalised. It is not unusual over time for services to reach a point where there are different releases of software, for example, that allow for similar functionality. Rationalisation enables services to be 'tidied up' and streamlined.

- **Refactor:** Services that provide more than one business outcome can be refactored to focus them on the one outcome. This may involve creating two services from one but each of the two services will be focused on the one business outcome.

- **Renew:** Services that deliver the required functionality but which need to be brought in line with the organisation's current technology requirements and architecture are renewed.

- **Retire:** Services that are no longer required because they no longer meet the business objectives of the organisation or of the customers.

Charter

The Charter phase of the Service Portfolio Management process is the final part. Decisions on services and funding are received and need to be checked and confirmed. Communication is the key: the chartered services represent the future strategy of the organisation and it is important that the messages accompanying the chartering of these services are understood and advertised. Once services are chartered the Service Portfolio is updated to reflect the change in status. For existing services, this will mean updates to the Service Catalogue; for future Services, the Service Pipeline will be updated. New or improved services then move to the Service Design phase of the IT Service Management Lifecycle while retiring services move to Service Transition and their subsequent removal from the Service Catalogue.

The anticipated value of each new or improved service will be known and the delivery and realisation of this value needs to be monitored throughout the lifecycle of the service. The monitoring should include financial reporting as well as resource utilisation assessments.

It can take a while to work all the way through the Service Portfolio Management process. It is a cycle and after Charter the circle turns back to Define. For some organisations this may be a quarterly or annual cycle for all existing and potential services or it may be triggered by changes in the environment in which the organisation operates. An individual service can be moved through the Service Portfolio Management lifecycle in response to a demand from the business areas or changes in legislation requiring new or updated services to meet revised regulatory standards.

8 SERVICE CATALOGUE MANAGEMENT

INTRODUCTION

The Service Catalogue Management process is responsible for the end-to-end management of the Service Catalogue. The Service Catalogue is part of the Service Portfolio and importantly it is visible to customers. This visibility to customers means that Service Catalogue Management is able to provide management of IT Services that is customer focused and in line with the needs of the business. The existence of a Service Catalogue also helps to develop a service focused approach within the IT Service Provider.

SERVICE CATALOGUE

A database or a structured document with information about all live IT Services, including those available for Deployment. The Service Catalogue is the only part of the Service Portfolio published to customers, and is used to support the sale and delivery of IT Services. The Service Catalogue includes information about deliverables, prices, contact points, ordering and request processes.

The Service Catalogue is customer focused so it is produced in business language that is accessible and understandable to customers. The services available are set out in a clear and consistent fashion. This allows an informed dialogue to take place between the IT Service Provider and the business areas around the available services where there is a clear and common understanding of the services and what they do and do not do. Having information on services that are available for deployment is also useful for business areas, giving them opportunities to adjust their short- and medium-term planning.

Clear business language gives customers an unambiguous view of what services are on offer. This is important, and it avoids any misunderstanding between the IT Service Provider and customers about the services actually offered. It also allows and facilitates discussions around the offerings.

As a consultant, I have facilitated a number of discussions between IT Service Providers and their customers where the aim was to arrive at an agreed understanding of the services in the Service Catalogue. By getting both the IT Service Provider representatives and the business area representatives to list separately what they believe to be the available services gives a useful starting point. Hopefully, the two lists are similar and, if they are, then it usually is an indication that there is a mature relationship in place with good communication channels and a common understanding of the services. Alternatively having similar lists may be a result of having a very straightforward set of services. However, it is the differences between the lists that often gives the more interesting insights.

A number of possibilities arise where the representatives of the IT Service Provider list a service that is not included by the business areas. Perhaps the service is not well advertised or maybe it has become obsolete from a business perspective. Further investigation is required to ensure that the IT Service Provider is not wasting resources and capabilities on producing and offering a service that does not have business demand.

Conversely, where the business area representatives list a service that is not included by the IT Service Provider, questions also need to be asked. It is not unusual for business areas to rely on a particular application in order to perform a business activity without the IT Service Provider realising that this is the case. This has obvious implications for availability and continuity. In my experience, IT Service Providers and business areas quite often find that yesterday's short-term tactical solution has become today's normal operation. This is why it is imperative that the IT Service Provider and the business areas have a shared view of what services are offered and received. This is what the Service Catalogue does.

It also helps if the Service Catalogue is integrated with the organisation's Configuration Management Database. Such integration provides a mechanism for linking the outward facing business-focused view of services with the inward looking technical view of services that incorporates all the components with their links and dependencies.

Service Catalogue information provides clarity on the business outcomes of the delivery of a single IT Service or a suite of IT Services. The information can also highlight the risks around the delivery of service that must be managed by the IT Service Provider. Service Catalogue information is a good starting point for Service Level Management when drawing up performance and cost reporting and is also important for Supplier Management in providing input for contract negotiation.

Business Service Catalogues and Technical Service Catalogues are discussed in more detail below. They are two aspects of the Service Catalogue with differing target audiences and focus. Where a Business Service Catalogue has been put in place the customers or business areas have a straightforward and easily understood mechanism for requesting services: a bit like selecting an item from a menu in a restaurant. A Business Service Catalogue will include details of the request and ordering processes. Adoption of a Technical Service Catalogue provides information that is more internal in focus, which allows the services to be managed more effectively and gives very useful input to Operational Level Agreements and third-party contracts.

PURPOSE, GOAL AND OBJECTIVES

Main book reference: SD 4.1.1

The purpose of Service Catalogue Management is to ensure that a single source of information presented in a consistent format is available to customers and business areas detailing information on all current services and those ready for deployment (i.e. those at the end of the Service Pipeline). The Service Catalogue must be easily accessible and available to those people and areas where access has been agreed. Service Catalogue Management is responsible for putting in place, updating, maintaining and managing the Service Catalogue. As well as being accessible, the Service Catalogue must meet the agreed requirements in terms of functionality, ease of use, availability and performance.

The goal of Service Catalogue Management is to make sure that an accurate and up-to-date Service Catalogue is in place and that it includes all current services and those ready for deployment. Once developed and in place, the Service Catalogue needs to be maintained to ensure that the information and services remain current and up to date.

The objectives of Service Catalogue Management are:

- To ensure that agreement is obtained with customers on the definition of a service and the format in which the Service Catalogue is to be presented. Accessibility, performance, functionality and performance requirements will need to be discussed, negotiated and agreed. The Service Catalogue is, in a sense, a marketing tool for the IT Service Provider and it is important to retain the balance between marketing and ensuring that the format and functionality meet the expectations of the customers and business areas.

- To design, develop, deploy and maintain the Service Catalogue in accordance with the business expectations that have been expressed in the form of requirements. The Service Catalogue has to fit and align with the rest of the Service Portfolio, and mechanisms need to be agreed within the wider Service Portfolio Management on triggers and interfaces for services moving into and out of the Service Catalogue.

- To ensure that the mechanisms agreed within the wider Service Portfolio Management on triggers and interfaces for services moving into and out of the Service Catalogue are implemented. There needs to be a clear handover process in place from the Service Pipeline to the Service Catalogue when services become ready for deployment in the live environment, and again a clear handover process in place when services move out of the Service Catalogue to be retired.

- To manage the Service Catalogue on a day-to-day basis to ensure that the agreed levels of performance, availability, functionality and accessibility are consistently delivered.

- To manage the information held within the Service Catalogue to ensure that the information made available to customers and business areas reflects the most up-to-date information available and to ensure that the information is presented in a consistent format. This information will include details of the status, interfaces and dependencies of all current services and those ready for deployment.

- To maintain and manage the Service Catalogue in accordance with robust change control in order to ensure that only up-to-date versions are available to customers and business areas. It is also important that the more internal facing Technical Service Catalogue is up to date with only current versions available. The use of an out-of-date Technical Service Catalogue would carry the same risks as using a Configuration Management Database that has not been updated in terms of not being able to understand fully current interfaces and dependencies.

- To work closely with Service Level Management as well as Business Relationship Management in order to ensure that the information contained and displayed in the Service Catalogue is correct and current.

- To work closely with Availability Management as well as IT Service Continuity Management and Security Management in order to ensure that the information contained and displayed in the Business Service Catalogue is correct and current.

- To work closely with Configuration Management in order to ensure that information, dependencies and interfaces detailed within the Technical Service Catalogue are correct and up to date. Input from Application Management, Technical Management, suppliers and support teams is required here.

THE SCOPE OF THE PROCESS

Main book reference: SD 4.1.2

The scope of the Service Catalogue Management process is to make information on all services delivered and those ready for deployment into the live environment available and accessible. The information must be up to date, consistent and accurate.

SCOPE

The boundary or extent to which a Process, procedure, certification, contract etc. applies. For example, the scope of the Change Management Process may include all live IT Services and related Configuration Items, the scope of an ISO/IEC 20000 certificate may include all IT Services delivered out of a named data centre.

The provision and maintenance of the Service Catalogue is a service in its own right and should have the attendant Service Level Agreements in place in order to ensure that the Service Catalogue meets business requirements in terms of performance, availability, functionality and accessibility. Additionally, the Service Level Agreements between the IT Service Provider and customers and business areas who use the Service Catalogue will include the provision for ensuring that the information contained within the Service Catalogue is up to date, consistent and accurate.

Service Catalogue Management is responsible for putting the Service Catalogue into operation in the first place. The Service Catalogue needs to be designed and its content agreed. The structure and accessibility, availability, functionality and performance of the Service Catalogue will need to be agreed as well as its content. The Service Catalogue is then developed and deployed with responsibilities and accountabilities in place to cover keeping it up to date. IT Service Continuity Management, IT Security Management, Access Management and audit procedures will need to be incorporated.

Agreed triggers and procedures will need to be in place across Service Portfolio Management to cover movement from the Service Pipeline to the Service Catalogue, and movement from the Service Catalogue to the depository for Retired Services. Outside Service Portfolio Management, the Service Catalogue's relationship and links with the Configuration Management Database will need to be agreed.

Once in operation, it is the responsibility of Service Catalogue Management to maintain the Service Catalogue. Ongoing Service Catalogue Management activities will include:

- maintaining and making available an up-to-date, accurate and consistent Service Catalogue;
- managing the information within the Service Catalogue to ensure that it is current, complete and relevant;
- ensuring that all services are properly defined within the Service Catalogue;
- responding to changing business requirements in relation to the Service Catalogue;
- responding to technology changes that may allow the IT Service Provider to alter how the Service Catalogue is populated, updated and presented (and how customers and business areas gain access to and view the Service Catalogue);
- managing the security, accessibility, availability, functionality and performance of the Service Catalogue in line with the agreed requirements;
- ensuring that the procedures for moving services in to and out of the Service Catalogue are adhered to and that triggers from within the wider Service Portfolio Management are responded to in relation to the migration of services;
- ensuring that the Service Catalogue information is consistent with the wider Service Portfolio information and that the interfaces and dependencies are managed;
- ensuring that the Service Catalogue remains aligned to the Configuration Management Database in accordance with the initial design of the Service Catalogue and that the interfaces and dependencies are managed.

THE INTERFACE TO THE SERVICE PORTFOLIO

Main book references: SD 3.6.2, 3.9, 3.10, SS 4.2.3

The Service Portfolio is the key management system in relation to managing all elements of services throughout their lifecycle. The Service Catalogue is the customer facing part of the Service Portfolio. When services are ready to be deployed in the live environment, it is the role of Service Catalogue Management to ensure that all information and details are accurate and up to date. At this stage Service Catalogue Management will work closely with Service Transition.

The Service Catalogue contains a subset of the services that are held within the Service Portfolio. In terms of the Service Portfolio Management lifecycle, the Service Catalogue contains those services that have been chartered and made ready for deployment and those services that are operational in the live environment. The Service Catalogue is the visible element of the Service Portfolio made available to customers. Customers will tend to be more focused on what the service provider is providing now or will be able to provide in the near future rather than what might be provided at some more distant future point. The Service Catalogue represents the Service Provider's current operational capability, while the Service Pipeline centres on future operational capability.

The Service Portfolio gives a full picture of an organisation's services. It is an overarching view of commitments and investments made by the service provider. Services planned and provided for all customers and in all markets are included. Information on services under development for future delivery is held in the Service Pipeline part of the Service Portfolio, while information on services in the live environment and those ready for live operation is held in the Service Catalogue part of the Service Portfolio. Information on retired services is also held within the Service Portfolio. The Service Catalogue section of the Service Portfolio sits between the Service Pipeline and Retired Services.

Financial control and governance is an important part of all of Service Portfolio Management. The Service Portfolio as a whole represents all the capabilities and resources across the phases of the IT Service Management lifecycle. However, it is the Service Catalogue that is the only part of the Service Portfolio that recovers costs or makes a profit.

THE DIFFERENCE BETWEEN A BUSINESS SERVICE CATALOGUE AND A TECHNICAL SERVICE CATALOGUE

Main book reference: SD 4.1.4

There are two aspects to a Service Catalogue. On the one hand it is used by customers and business areas to select services that are appropriate to delivering their business objectives. On the other hand it allows internal areas of the IT Service Provider to view and understand how a service is delivered and the components that underpin that delivery. Many organisations divide their Service

Catalogue into a Business Service Catalogue and a Technical Service Catalogue so both aspects are reflected.

Business Service Catalogue

The services are set out and described in a business-oriented manner. All the IT services delivered to customers are included as well as the links and relationships between the services and the business processes they support. This is the aspect of the Service Catalogue that is aimed at and available to customers. The Business Service Catalogue lets the customers and business areas (as well as potential customers) view the services provided by the IT Service Provider in a way that makes it easy for them to understand which services they use. It also lets them assess which services may be appropriate for them in the future.

It is important that the Business Service Catalogue is user-friendly and that it is designed in collaboration with customers in order to ensure that the contents and presentation meet their requirements. Use of the Business Service Catalogue lets the IT Service Provider be more proactive in its relationships with the business areas.

Technical Service Catalogue

The services are set out and described in a technical manner. This is the IT perspective with all services and components described in IT terms. All the IT services delivered to customers are included as well as the links and relationships between the services and the links and relationships with supporting components and Configuration Items. This technical view of the services is not made available to customers. It is used internally within the IT Service Provider in order to enhance the understanding of how services fit together and how they are made up.

The Technical Service Catalogue is very useful for Service Level Management when they are looking at the components that underpin services and identifying the need for Operational Level Agreements and Underpinning Contracts. It is a good idea to record details of key personnel who are responsible for particular components. However, this should be limited to key personnel only because it should always be borne in mind that the more information that is held, the greater the maintenance overhead will be.

Ideally the Business Service Catalogue and the Technical Service Catalogue will be two aspects of one integrated Service Catalogue. However, some organisations only maintain either a Business Service Catalogue or a Technical Service Catalogue. Organisations with a number of diverse customers, or organisations that operate in more than one market, may have more than one Service Catalogue. Where this is the case, each Service Catalogue is a reflection of the organisation's operational capability in respect of that customer or market. Each Service Catalogue is a projection from the Service Portfolio.

The use of the two aspects of the Service Catalogue together lets the IT Service Provider quickly understand and map the impact of Incidents, Problems and Changes on the business areas. The Technical Service Catalogue highlights which components are or may be impacted, while the Business Service Catalogue highlights the impact on business processes.

THE IMPORTANCE TO THE SERVICE LIFECYCLE AND TO THE BUSINESS

Main book references: SS 4.2.3, SD 3.10, 4.1.3

The Service Catalogue contributes value to the business areas by providing a consolidated single source of information on all the services delivered by the IT Service Provider. This enables all business areas and all parts of the business areas to view consistent, accurate and up-to-date information on all the services they currently receive and those they could potentially receive in the future. The Business Service Catalogue in particular provides a business perspective on the services being delivered including highlighting all the links to business processes. The inclusion of Service Level Management information within the Service Catalogue lets the business areas understand the levels of service and the quality of service available for each service delivered.

The Service Catalogue plays an important role throughout the Service Lifecycle. Service Strategy and Service Design use it to help develop and advertise offerings and as a projection of the IT Service Provider's capabilities to the business areas. Services moving in to or out of the Service Catalogue will come under the remit of Service Transition.

Service Operation will use the Technical Service Catalogue in particular in order to assess the impact of Changes, Incidents and Problems on the infrastructure and on the services that the infrastructure underpins. The Business Service Catalogue then allows these impacts to be mapped against the business processes served by the services.

Continual Service Improvement can often be triggered by issues identified in either the Business Service Catalogue or the Technical Service Catalogue. Services set out such that they are understandable from both a business and a technical perspective allow opportunities for improvement to be more readily identified.

IT Service Management as a whole brings a holistic approach to the delivery of service. It breaks down the traditional 'stovepipes' within IT and focuses more on processes across the individual IT teams. The Service Catalogue is a good example of this because it highlights how components are combined in order to provide services. Consequently, individual IT teams, which were previously 'islands' of expertise and knowledge, can more easily understand how their contribution fits into the delivery of services to the business areas. This benefits the IT Service Provider as well as its customers in the business areas.

Business Service Management is all about ensuring that the links between IT components, services and the goals of the business areas are understood. Business Service Management is particularly interested in the impact of IT and IT changes on the business. Conversely, the business is also interested in the impact of business changes on the IT infrastructure.

The Service Catalogue is a critical tool for Business Service Management in these regards. Business Service Management can only really deliver if there is a well-maintained, accurate and up-to-date comprehensive Service Catalogue in place. Business Service Management's proactive use of the Service Catalogue will enable improvements to be made in the alignment of the provision of IT services with the needs of the business areas now and in the future.

POLICIES, PRINCIPLES AND BASIC CONCEPTS

Main book reference: SD 4.1.4

The Service Catalogue contains information on all services that are being delivered by Service Operation as well as all those services that are ready and approved to be transitioned into production. Importantly, the Service Catalogue is visible to customers. The Service Catalogue represents the service provider's current capability. The Service Catalogue can be used to provide solutions for customers that are made up of more than one service. Third-party services may be included in the Service Catalogue and offered direct to customers as they are or with enhancements.

The Service Catalogue should be integrated with the Configuration Management Database. Integration would enable a holistic view to be taken of the outward customer-facing Service Catalogue together with the internal components that make up the services. Additionally, critical areas of the infrastructure on which live services depend would be easily highlighted. Integration would allow a particular service to be viewed both from an external business perspective and from an internal technical perspective. The Technical Service Catalogue, in particular, is very dependent on the availability of accurate and up-to-date Configuration information.

The Service Catalogue section of the Service Portfolio sits between the Service Pipeline and Retired Services and represents the IT Service Provider's current capability. When services are ready and approved for transition into the live environment, they move from the Service Pipeline to the Service Catalogue.

When services are no longer required, they are transitioned from the Service Catalogue to Retired Services. A service may be retired because it is no longer demanded, it is no longer economical to operate, it is no longer cost-effective or it has been superseded by another service. There may be occasions where a service meets some or all of these reasons for retirement but where the IT Service Provider wishes to retain it in the Service Catalogue (e.g. a service that acts as continuity for another critical service). The level and amount of information retained when a service is retired should be driven by a decision on what it would be useful to keep (in terms of the service being used again or in terms of information that would be useful for other potential future services).

The services within the Service Catalogue are split or grouped into Lines of Business in order to bring similar and complementary services together and to help customers more easily identify what fits with the demand that they have. The Lines of Business groupings are matched with the Patterns of Business Activity that they can support. The adoption of Lines of Business groupings within the Service Catalogue makes it easier to identify which areas are performing better than others, thereby allowing resources to be allocated in line with the more successful and growing services and markets.

Third-party services are a grouping or subset of services often seen within a Service Catalogue. These services may be offered in the form that they have been bought in or may be enhanced by the IT Service Provider. Third-party services are sometimes used if there is insufficient current capability to match demand. When this is the case, the third-party services are used as an interim measure until new services can progress through the Service Pipeline and into the Service Catalogue. Likewise, third-party services may also be used where services have been retired as demand reduces and where it no longer makes economical or strategic sense for the IT Service Provider to produce them in-house.

Having services within the Service Catalogue ties up resources and capabilities, which is why it is crucial that an organisation continually reviews the contents of its Service Catalogue and the wider Service Portfolio. Services that are not performing well may be identified as candidates for removal from the Service Catalogue. However, this may not be a straightforward decision because the delivery of the services may be committed contractually for a further period or they may provide contingency for other services.

It is important to monitor continually service performance from a financial perspective. This financial monitoring should take into consideration the original business case together with benefits realisation to date, and potential and expected future benefits realisation.

Organisations will strive to make the best use of resources and the Service Portfolio allows areas where components can be standardised and reused across services to be highlighted. This avoids duplication of cost and effort where very similar components are required for different services. The more components that are standardised and reused, the more the organisation can leverage economies of scale and reduce the cost of producing each extra unit of a component.

The Service Catalogue is the only part of the Service Portfolio that includes services in the live environment. Therefore, Service Transition is involved when services move in to and out of the Service Catalogue. This ensures that services that are live can be fully supported. It is also critical that Service Transition is involved in managing any changes to services within the Service Catalogue. Once a service is in the Service Catalogue and operational it will be relied on by customers and there will often be a contractual obligation to deliver.

Compiling a Service Catalogue from scratch can be time-consuming. It may be difficult to obtain all the necessary information. The history and ownership of some services could be difficult to ascertain. It is always informative to under-stand what services the business believes it receives and compare it with what the IT Service Provider believes that it delivers.

Organisations should develop and maintain a policy for the Service Catalogue con-cerning exactly what details are recorded for each service as well as which statuses.

The responsibilities for all stages of Service Catalogue Management will also be recorded in the policy document.

KEY METRICS, CHALLENGES, CRITICAL SUCCESS FACTORS AND RISKS

Main book references: SD 4.1.8, 4.1.9

The Service Catalogue Management process has two important Key Performance Indicators. These are:

- the percentage of services being delivered that are recorded and managed in the Service Catalogue;
- the number of incidences of variances being identified between the information held within the Service Catalogue and the actual situation with regards to the service.

KEY PERFORMANCE INDICATOR

A metric that is used to help manage a Process, IT Service or an Activity. Many metrics may be measured but only the most important metrics are defined as Key Performance Indicators (KPIs) and are used to manage and report actively on the Process, IT Service or Activity. KPIs should be selected to ensure that efficiency, effectiveness and cost-effectiveness are all managed.

There also needs to be metrics in relation to the level of adoption of the Service Catalogue both within the business areas and internally within the IT Service Provider. Metrics in this area may include:

- percentage increase in the inclusion in the Business Service Catalogue of all services and their links and interfaces to the business processes;
- percentage increase in the inclusion in the Technical Service Catalogue of all services and their links and interfaces to the underpinning components and infrastructure.

METRIC

Something that is measured and reported on to help manage a Process, IT Service or Activity.

The fundamental challenge that Service Catalogue Management has to surmount is the need to create a comprehensive Service Catalogue and then to maintain the

Service Catalogue to ensure that it remains comprehensive, up to date and accurate. This is not easy and the degree of the task will be dependent on the size and complexity of the IT Service Provider and the business areas that are its customers.

Maintaining the Technical Service Catalogue aspect of the Service Catalogue requires close liaison with all the internal technical areas within the IT Service Provider as well as with external third-party suppliers. The links and relationships between all the components and infrastructure that make up services need to be understood and recorded. There needs to be buy-in throughout the IT Service Provider with regards to the value that the Technical Service Catalogue brings.

Maintaining the Business Service Catalogue aspect of the Service Catalogue requires close working with the business areas in order to ensure that the impact of services on business processes are fully understood and recorded. Business areas will be keen to use the Business Service Catalogue if they can see that it provides value to them when analysing how they deliver their business processes now, how they might deliver them in the future and what other options there may be.

Updating the Service Catalogue is made easier if it forms part of the Configuration Management System and the Service Knowledge Management System. An integrated approach to the population and maintenance of the databases will reduce the risks of duplication of effort and failure to understand and react to dependencies.

The key Critical Success Factors (CSFs) for the Service Catalogue Management process are:

- an up-to-date, accurate and consistent Service Catalogue;
- business users and business areas being aware of the services being made available by the IT Service Provider;
- business users and business areas being aware of the links between the services provided by the IT Service Provider and the business processes;
- internal IT staff being aware of the services being made available by the IT Service Provider;
- internal IT staff being aware of the links between the services provided by the IT Service Provider and the underpinning components and infrastructure.

CRITICAL SUCCESS FACTOR

Something that must happen if a Process, project, plan or IT Service is to succeed. Key Performance Indicators (KPIs) are used to measure the achievement of each Critical Success Factor. For example, a Critical Success Factor of 'protect IT Services when making changes' could be measured by KPIs such as 'percentage reduction of unsuccessful changes', 'percentage reduction in changes causing Incidents' etc.

The risks associated with the Service Catalogue Management process are:

- The Service Catalogue is not accurate and up to date.
- The Service Catalogue does not have a high enough profile within the business areas, where key stakeholders are not aware of its existence or contents.
- It is not easy for the business areas to link the services being provided by the IT Service Provider with the business processes.
- The inability to obtain accurate and up-to-date information from the IT Support areas.
- The Service Catalogue does not have a high enough profile within the internal IT Support areas, where staff are not aware of its existence or contents.
- It is not easy for the IT Support areas to link the services being provided by the IT Service Provider with the underpinning components and infrastructure.
- The Service Catalogue is not consistent.
- The inability to obtain accurate and up-to-date information from the business areas.
- The lack of resources to undertake the tasks and roles of Service Catalogue Management.
- The inability to obtain accurate and up-to-date information from the Service Portfolio.
- Change control is not exerted on the Service Catalogue.
- The lack of tools to undertake the tasks and roles of Service Catalogue Management.
- The inability to gain access to accurate and up-to-date Configuration Management information and Service Knowledge Management information.
- The Service Catalogue is bypassed in discussions and decision-making processes taking place between IT Service Provider staff and the business areas.
- The level of information within the Service Catalogue is too high to allow meaningful analysis to take place.
- The level of information within the Service Catalogue is too low to allow it to be maintained in an accurate and timely fashion.

ACTIVITIES AND USE BY OTHER PROCESSES AND FUNCTIONS

Main book references: SD 4.1.5, 4.1.6

The main activities of the Service Catalogue Management process are:

- Discussing, developing, agreeing and documenting a definition of a service. This should take place with all key stakeholders at the outset. It is important that it is correct from the outset because lack of clarity on what constitutes a service is the most common cause of a Service Catalogue lacking the required profile both within the business areas and internally with the IT Service Provider.

- Designing, developing and maintaining the Service Catalogue as a part of the wider Service Portfolio. Agreement will need to be reached with Service Portfolio Management on the contents of both the Service Portfolio and the Service Catalogue.

- Working with Service Portfolio Management to agree the triggers and interfaces that should exist between the Service Pipeline and the Service Catalogue as well as the triggers and interfaces that should exist between the Service Catalogue and Retired Services.

- Maintaining the Service Catalogue under strict Change Control. Additionally, the Service Catalogue should be subject to robust version control with only the current versions available and in circulation. The existence and reliance on out-of-date versions would quickly lead to lack of confidence in the Service Catalogue.

- Maintaining the Business Service Catalogue by regularly liaising with business areas to ensure that the contents remain aligned to the business processes.

- Regularly liaising with Service Level Management, Business Relationship Management, Service Portfolio Management and Service Continuity Management to ensure that the Business Service Catalogue continues to reflect the current situation with regard to the services and their links and relationships with the business processes.

- Maintaining the Technical Service Catalogue by regularly liaising with the internal IT Support teams and suppliers to ensure that the contents remain valid in relation to the existing components and infrastructure.

- Regularly liaising with Configuration Management, Service Continuity Management and suppliers to ensure that the Business Service Catalogue continues to reflect the current situation with regards to the services and their links and relationships with the underpinning components and infrastructure.

- Managing the Service Catalogue so that all services in operation as well as new services moving into transition are accurately recorded. Retired Services should be removed from the Service Catalogue as and when appropriate.

- Undertaking ongoing dialogue with the key stakeholders in order to ensure that the Service Catalogue remains valid and continues to meet the requirements of its audience.

The Service Catalogue is used by a number of other processes and functions:

- **Service Portfolio Management:** The Service Catalogue forms part of the Service Portfolio, so the two processes must work in unison to ensure that there is a common definition of services and a clear understanding of the triggers and processes for services moving from the Service Pipeline, to the Service Catalogue and finally to retirement.

- **Financial Management:** Information from the Service Catalogue is used by Financial Management to produce plans and budgets. This is particularly important in the area of service demand. Financial Management can understand the cost of services by using the Service Catalogue to understand how services fit together. The Business Service Catalogue gives an insight into the value of services to the business area. Useful comparisons can then be made both between services and between alternative methods of providing services. Benchmarking of services with those produced by competitors is also possible.

- **Service Continuity Management:** Information derived from the Service Catalogue can be used by Service Continuity Management to perform Business Impact Analysis as part of IT Service Continuity Planning.

- **Business Continuity Management:** This will use Service Catalogue information to perform Business Impact Analysis and identify Vital Business Functions.

- **Capacity Management:** Information from the Service Catalogue will help Capacity Management by providing the raw materials to start to look at workloads across services with the intention of redistributing the workloads in a more efficient manner.

- **Configuration Management:** For organisations without a Configuration Management Database, the Service Catalogue provides a good starting point for its development. For organisations with a Service Catalogue integrated with the Configuration Management System, the impact of Incidents, Problems and Changes can quickly be ascertained in relation to services and the business processes that those services support. If the Service Catalogue and the Configuration Management System are not integrated, duplicate information on the Configuration Items will be held leading to a greater maintenance overhead and a greater risk of inconsistent information within the organisation.

- **Change Management:** Information about the potential impact of future changes on services and the business processes they support can be derived from the Service Catalogue.

- **Availability Management:** The work on the creation of a Projected Service Outages document is helped considerably by having Service Catalogue details of all services, their Service Level Agreements (SLAs), details of underpinning components and infrastructure, and the links to business processes.

PRODUCING A SERVICE CATALOGUE

Main book reference: SD Appendix G

The Service Catalogue should include information on all services and their status as they move through the Service Lifecycle. The Service Catalogue is customer facing so it should contain information that is useful to customers and should be presented in such a way as to be easily accessible and usable.

For each service the information shown in Table 8.1 should be displayed.

Table 8.1 Contents of the Service Catalogue

	SERVICE A	SERVICE B	SERVICE C	SERVICE D
NAME OF SERVICE				
SERVICE DESCRIPTION				
SERVICE TYPE				
SERVICE STATUS				
SERVICE OWNER				
SERVICE MANAGER				
BUSINESS OWNER				
BUSINESS UNIT/UNITS				
BUSINESS CONTACTS				
SUPPORTING SERVICES				
SERVICE LEVEL AGREEMENT				
AVAILABILITY				
SUPPORT ARRANGEMENTS				
BUSINESS IMPACT				
BUSINESS PRIORITY				
SERVICE HOURS				
ESCALATION CONTACTS				
SERVICE REPORTS				
SERVICE REVIEWS				
SECURITY DETAILS				
KEY FUTURE PLANS, ORDERING AND CANCELLATION				
COSTS AND CHARGING				
TERMS AND CONDITIONS				

9 SERVICE LEVEL MANAGEMENT

INTRODUCTION

This chapter covers the Service Level Management process and its deliverables. Service Level Management (SLM) is the prime interface between the IT Service Provider and the business. SLM ensures that business requirements are fully understood and then encapsulated and translated into meaningful agreements with targets allowing the delivery of IT Services to be aligned with business needs.

SERVICE LEVEL MANAGEMENT

The Process responsible for negotiating Service Level Agreements, and ensuring that these Service Level Agreements are met. Service Level Management is responsible for ensuring that all IT Service Management Processes, Operational Level Agreements and Underpinning Contracts are appropriate for the agreed Service Level Targets. Service Level Management monitors and reports on Service Levels, and holds regular reviews with customers.

It is crucial that Service Levels Targets and Service Level Agreements (SLAs) reflect the requirements of the business and match the expectations of the customers in terms of availability, performance and functionality.

SERVICE LEVEL

A measured and reported achievement against one or more Service Level Targets. The term Service Level is sometimes used informally to mean Service Level Target.

SLM is responsible for negotiating, agreeing and documenting Service Targets for IT with business representatives. These agreed Service Targets are incorporated into a SLA or SLAs. All IT Services need to be incorporated into this process. Once Agreements are in place SLM is responsible for monitoring and reporting on performance against the Service Targets set out in the SLAs.

IT SERVICE PROVIDER

A Service Provider that provides IT Services to internal customers or external customers.

The existence of properly agreed, documented and understood Agreements significantly reduces the risk of the IT Service Provider delivering a service that is not what the business actually wanted or required. In this respect SLM acts as a bridge between the IT Service Provider and the business and is the focal point for this critical relationship. Maintaining the relationship with the business areas is an important SLM activity. The relationship needs to be managed and constructive: good communication is essential.

Continual Service Improvement is something else that is fundamental to the SLM process. The SLM process must ensure that services 'do not stand still', although improvements need to be what the business require and cost justified.

SLM makes sure that the SLAs that are put in place are underpinned by the necessary Operational Level Agreements (OLAs) and Underpinning Contracts (UCs) to ensure that all aspects of the delivery of the service are fully understood, documented and managed.

PURPOSE, GOAL AND OBJECTIVES

Main book reference: SD 4.2.1

The goal of SLM is to ensure that levels of IT Service delivered to customers are negotiated, agreed and documented. The agreed levels of IT Service are then delivered to customers with measurements in place to demonstrate delivery. These measurements are also agreed with the business areas and are set out in a way that can be understood in relation to the service (i.e. not in technical jargon). The measurements should be reported by SLM to the business areas on a regular basis.

The purpose of SLM is to ensure that the services delivered fully align with the needs of the business. Regular communication and monitoring help SLM in the fulfilment of this purpose.

The SLM objectives are:

- To set out, document, negotiate and agree levels of IT Service provided to business areas.
- To monitor, measure and report on the agreed levels of IT Service provided to business areas.
- To manage the performance of services so that agreed levels of service are delivered, monitored and reported.

- To review service regularly with a view to improving continually the level of service available subject to business agreement and financial considerations. SLM conducts the monitoring and measuring of service so it is in an ideal position to drive service improvement in partnership with the business areas.

- To build and maintain effective relationships with customers bringing about trust and transparency.

- To work closely with business areas to monitor customer satisfaction and to increase proactively levels of customer satisfaction.

- To advertise and raise awareness of the process and the SLAs in order to make sure that there is a clear understanding within the IT Service Provider and within the business areas on what levels of service should be delivered and expected.

THE SCOPE OF THE PROCESS

Main book reference: SD 4.2.2

The scope of the SLM process is all the current services delivered by the IT Service Provider to the business areas as well as planned new services. SLM must ensure that all business areas are represented and that all parts of the IT Service Provider are engaged and aware (particularly in relation to their OLA responsibilities).

Where new services are planned or where services are to be changed, it is important that SLM obtains and agrees new or revised Service Level Requirements.

In order to manage the delivery of service, the SLM process needs:

- To obtain, negotiate and agree business requirements.

- To document, manage, monitor, measure and report on all SLAs for existing services.

- To understand, document and agree future business requirements for new or altered services.

- To ensure that all SLAs have the necessary underpinning OLA and UCs in place and to ensure that these underpinning OLA and UCs are managed, monitored, measured and reported on.

- To build and maintain relationships with business areas.

- To work closely with areas such as Problem Management, Capacity Management and Availability Management to prevent proactively loss of service or degraded service. Where service failures do occur, SLM will be involved in driving and prioritising speedy restoration of service through the Incident Management process.

- To highlight and raise awareness of breaks in service as well as identifying and illuminating parts of a service (both within the IT Service Provider and the business areas) that are vulnerable to failure.

- To ensure that Continual Service Improvement is in place for all services and is managed through Service Improvement Plans.

THE VALUE TO THE SERVICE LIFECYCLE AND TO THE BUSINESS

Main book references: SD 4.2 up to 4.2.1, 4.2.3

SLM plays a key role in the Service Lifecycle. SLM is able to ensure that the necessary frameworks are in place to deliver the service when it is introduced and through its operational life because it is engaged when Service Level Requirements are being formed, discussed and agreed for new or changed services. This structured approach aims to ensure all aspects of the operation of the service throughout its life are taken into account from the outset.

SLM provides business value by providing the business areas with their focal point for the supply of services. The provision of SLM provides an assurance to the business areas that their services are being managed and monitored. Regular reporting further demonstrates this management and monitoring. Where failures in service do occur, SLM provides a visible interface providing information on the failure, remedial action and future preventative action.

PRINCIPLES AND BASIC CONCEPTS

Main book reference: SD 4.2.4

The key concept of SLM is the provision of a bridge between the IT Service Provider and the business areas. SLM provides the focal point for the business areas in their dealings with the IT Service Provider. The converse is also true in that SLM provides the focal point for the various sections and areas of the IT Service Provider in their dealings with the business areas. Communication is the key to the relationship between the IT Service Provider and the business areas and SLM is the route for this communication. The role of Service Manager provides an identifiable individual responsible for a service.

SERVICE MANAGER

A manager who is responsible for managing the end-to-end lifecycle of one or more IT Services. The term Service Manager is also used to mean any manager within the IT Service Provider. The term Service Manager is most commonly used to refer to a Business Relationship Manager, a Process Manager, an Account Manager or a senior manager with responsibility for IT Services overall.

SLM is predominately involved with managing current services, but it is also involved in ensuring new requirements or changed requirements are also picked up as early as possible from the business areas. This enables SLM to take a holistic view of how future requirements and services will map out and allows the implications for existing services to be taken into account.

IT SERVICE

A Service provided to one or more customers by an IT Service Provider. An IT Service is based on the use of information technology and supports the customer's business processes. An IT Service is made up from a combination of people, processes and information technology and should be defined in a Service Level Agreement.

The SLM activities of planning, drafting, negotiating, agreeing, managing and performance monitoring of SLAs forms a foundation for the delivery of service and provides SLM with the tools to perform the role as the focal point between the IT Service Provider and the business areas.

Figure 9.1 shows SLM acting as the bridge and focal point between the IT Service Provider and the Business. SLM represents the IT Service Provider to the Business and also represents the Business areas to the IT Service Provider.

Figure 9.1 The SLM relationship between the IT Service Provider and the Business
(Source: OGC ITIL Service Design ISBN 978-0-113310-47-0)

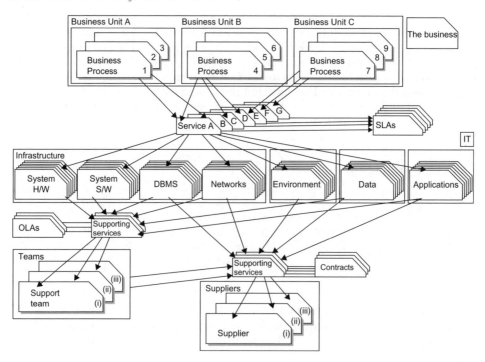

It is key that SLM builds strong relationships built on trust and proven delivery in both directions. In this way expectations are understood and managed.

The SLA as a clear, concise and unambiguous document is the vehicle used by SLM to manage services. SLM is responsible for ensuring that each SLA is underpinned by the necessary OLAs incorporating the required technical descriptions and UC with third parties containing the legal provisions and recourses.

PROCESS ACTIVITIES, METHODS AND TECHNIQUES

Main book references: SD 4.2.5 up to 4.2.5.3, including Figures 4.5, 4.6, 4.7

This section includes the Service Level Agreement Structures and the determination of Service Level Requirements.

A number of activities and subprocesses make up the overall SLM process. These are:

- Deriving, negotiating, documenting and agreeing the business needs (requirements) for new or altered services. These are set out as Service Level Requirements and their delivery is dependent on identification and negotiation with the correct business area(s).

- Documenting, negotiating and agreeing the underpinning OLAs. These need to be in place before a final commitment is given to the SLA. Organisations must ensure that they have the underlying capability to deliver before entering into a final commitment. Many SLAs will require a network or web of OLAs and third-party UCs to be in place in order for the IT Service Provider to be able to deliver with confidence.

- Documenting, negotiating and agreeing the UCs in conjunction with Supplier Management. As with the OLAs, the UCs with third parties should be in place prior to the final commitment on the SLA.

- Documenting, negotiating and agreeing the SLAs.

- Deciding on the appropriate structure for a SLA framework for the organisation. This will be dependent on the size, complexity and diversity of the organisation and the services together with the maturity of and levels of collaboration within and between both the IT Service Provider and the business areas.

- Proactively managing and monitoring the actual service performance of all services covered by SLAs (which ought to be all operational services). Again, the ability and capability to monitor, manage and report on service performance needs to be in place prior to the final commitment to the SLA. The monitoring may take place in various parts of the IT Service Provider and beyond, and the activities will be included in the OLAs and UCs for third parties. SLM is responsible for pulling together the OLA and UC Reporting. It then takes a holistic view across the service prior to reporting on service performance to the business areas.

- Obtaining information on customer satisfaction and using this information to trigger and drive proactive continual service improvement.

- Organising and conducting regular service review meetings with the parties to the SLA. An agenda should be distributed and minutes taken and sent out highlighting areas for future focus and improvement. Reviews should include the scope or extent of the Service as well as Requirements, OLAs and UCs.

- Setting up and managing Service Improvements Plans.

- Managing and monitoring all the OLAs that underpin the SLA.

- Managing and monitoring, in conjunction with Supplier Management, all the UCs that support the SLA.

- Developing the relationship with the business areas who are party to the SLA. This includes increasing levels of trust, communication and collaboration.

- Reporting on all Service performance and proactively managing the Service throughout its lifecycle. This includes the provision of management information to allow performance to be measured and managed.

- Developing and maintaining the standards and documents for the SLM process. This includes making available the document templates for SLAs, OLAs and UCs.

- Putting in place a process for handling complaints (and compliments). This will involve logging, managing and reporting on complaints.

- Improving the SLM process. SLM is responsible for improving the services, but it is also responsible for ensuring that the process itself is subject to continual improvement. Metrics can be used to illustrate this. A common measure of SLM performance is percentage of SLAs, OLAs and UCs reviewed in the last X months.

Figure 9.2 illustrates the main activities of SLM. SLM is the combination of all of these activities or subprocesses. The activities need to be brought together to create a coherent approach and SLM process.

Service Level Requirements

The business needs for a particular service or group of services must be gathered. These are the business requirements. The business requirement for a particular service should be set out in the Service Level Requirement (SLR).

SERVICE LEVEL REQUIREMENT

A customer requirement for an aspect of an IT Service. Service Level Requirements (SLRs) are based on business objectives and used to negotiate agreed Service Level Targets.

Figure 9.2 The main activities of SLM (Source: OGC ITIL Service Design ISBN 978-0-113310-47-0)

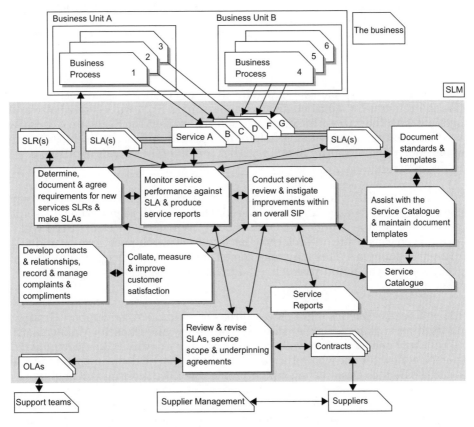

It is crucial that the IT Service Provider is in dialogue with the correct part or parts of the business. IT departments are sometimes accused (often fairly) of being made up of disparate groups who do not communicate well with each other and do not fully understand the role of other groups within their overall area. The same often applies to business areas. The term 'the business' is often heard, but in reality it is not always easy to identify the correct part of the business to discuss and negotiate with.

SLM must identify that part of the business or the spokesperson for all the areas who is in a position to negotiate. It should be the area with the business responsibility for the service and, crucially, the area with the budgetary control for the service. Failure to identify and negotiate with the correct area of the business can lead to avoidable delays and unrecoverable costs.

Business requirements will be set out in the terms that the business areas use and understand in relation to a Service. These are the Business needs and will include targets for both availability and performance.

The Business areas should be engaged as early as possible. This helps to engender trust and reduces the risk of expectations that cannot be fulfilled. Often a business area will know exactly what it wants, but this is not always the case. SLM may guide the business areas towards what is possible, but it must be careful not to be seen to be imposing a particular service solution. SLM should use a standard SLR template and then work with the business areas to populate that template.

Often, more than one business area is involved and their wishes, expectations and requirements for a particular service may differ. SLM will need to liaise and negotiate with the various business areas to ensure that the SLRs are a consolidated business requirement. It is helpful if somebody within the Business has the responsibility and authority to pull together the different strands of business requirements.

Building up the SLRs is an iterative process. SLM will need to ensure that what is being specified can actually be delivered. Delivery will require the OLAs and Contracts to be able to underpin what is being requested, therefore SLM will need to keep consulting and referring back to internal Support groups and to third-party suppliers. This may take some time, but it is crucial so that the agreed service can actually be delivered in terms of availability, performance and cost.

SLM will need to include other process areas in addition to the Support Groups and third-party Suppliers. For example, Availability and Capacity Management will certainly need to be involved, as will IT Service Continuity Management. A potential new service where Incident handling is particularly important would lead to the Service Desk having a high-profile role in supporting and helping SLM in the negotiations. Change and Release Management will be involved with the introduction of a new service and ongoing changes, and will want to ensure that their needs are understood and met. Likewise, Financial Management must be engaged from the outset.

So SLM is pulling together, coordinating and managing a number of strands when discussing and deriving SLRs. All these inputs must be balanced. Not only is SLM in discussion with the business areas, but also with:

- Internal Support Groups (e.g. Applications Management teams and Database Management groups).
- Third-party Suppliers (e.g. outsourced Networks teams or bespoke application software suppliers).
- Process areas within the IT Service Provider (e.g. Availability, Capacity and IT Service Continuity Management).
- Other impacted or dependent areas (e.g. Facilities Management).

All of this can be time-consuming, but it is crucial that the SLRs are correct at the start so that unfulfilled expectations are avoided and the risk of costly future upgrades is reduced.

The implications of the introduction of a new Service must be fully understood and managed. This is not just the implications for the Service itself, but also for other existing or planned services and all the support teams (both internal and external) as well as other IT Service Management processes. The SLR will be outlined as part of the Service Design criteria and then improved and updated through an iterative process throughout the lifecycle of the service. Service Transition activities such as testing will provide a useful and crucial check on the SLRs and allow improvements to be highlighted and then made.

The degree to which third-party Suppliers are to be involved in producing and providing the service will determine the level of involvement of Procurement and Supplier Management in developing the SLRs. It may be that a tendering process reveals cost implications that alter how a service is sourced and provided. The involvement of other groups outside SLM and the business areas may remain constant, reduce or increase as the SLRs develop and mature.

Frameworks for SLAs

Services provided by an IT Service Provider are often shared by more than one customer. Likewise customers will use a number of services. This allows different structures or frameworks to be put in place in order to manage the SLAs between the IT Service Provider and its customers.

Customer-based Service Level Agreements

A customer-based SLA is an agreement with a specific customer covering all the services that they use. The advantage of this approach is that all services that a customer uses are covered in one document.

An example of a customer-based SLA would be a training department, which would sign up to a single agreement covering email, administration systems, human resources, intranet, as well as specific training systems. Such SLAs can quickly become quite complicated and they need to be carefully managed. There may be frustrations for users because while some systems are bespoke and tailored to their requirements, others, such as email or intranet, are not.

Service-based Service Level Agreements

A service-based SLA is an agreement put in place with all customers of a particular service. This approach is appropriate where all customers expect and receive the same level of service (e.g. email or intranet). This seems straightforward; however, it is often the case that services are not the same for all users due to location and their immediate infrastructure.

A service-based SLA approach can be a pragmatic response to an environment where there are multiple users, but often the users will demand differing levels of service. Some organisations offer different banded levels of service or support within a service-based SLA in order to combat this issue (e.g. silver, gold and platinum).

Another potential issue with service-based SLAs is identifying a signatory to the SLA who is able to represent all customers and users across an organisation. Although there should be an identifiable individual or individuals taking the signing responsibility, the use of user groups or champions is a useful approach to ensure that all areas feel involved and are represented.

Multilevel Service Level Agreements

Multilevel SLAs are in layers and are usually made up of corporate-level SLAs, customer-level SLAs and service-level SLAs (see Figure 9.3).

Figure 9.3 Multilevel Service Level Agreement (Source: OGC ITIL Service Design ISBN 978-0-113310-47-0)

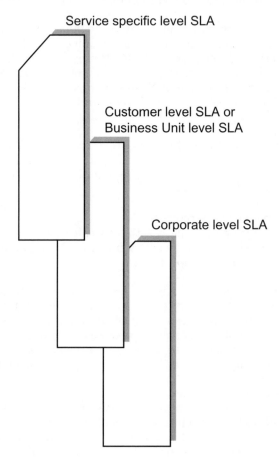

- Services that are common to all customers are covered at the corporate level. These tend to be established and stable services.

- All services that are applicable to a particular customer are included at the customer level.

- All issues relating to a specific service for a customer are covered at the service level.

There will be an overlap between the corporate level and the customer level as illustrated in the diagram. There will also be an overlap between the customer level and the service level.

It is important that, despite the different levels, the links to the Service Catalogue and the Configuration Management System are maintained.

Service Level Agreements

The Service Level Agreement (SLA) is the mechanism used by Service Level Management to manage the relationship between itself as the IT Service Provider and the business areas who are its customers.

SERVICE LEVEL AGREEMENT (SLA)

An agreement between an IT Service Provider and a customer. The SLA describes the IT Service, records Service Level Targets, and specifies the responsibilities for the IT Service Provider and the customer. A single SLA may cover multiple IT Services or multiple customers.

The wording of SLAs should be clear, concise and unambiguous. They should be written in business language and should not contain overly technical or legal phraseology. Technical language is appropriate for OLAs, while legal language should be included in third-party contracts. Often SLAs will cover different countries and may need to be translated, and this is another driver for keeping the original language clear, concise and unambiguous.

In order to be effective, the SLA must be agreed and signed by all the parties that it impacts. The SLA sets out exactly what is to be delivered, when it is to be delivered, how it is to be delivered and where it is to be delivered, and all of this is documented in such a way that easily makes sense to the customer. The responsibilities of both the IT Service Provider and the customer will be clearly set out and levels of performance, availability and access will be detailed. The customer responsibilities are particularly important in the area of access to the service. They will set out who can use the service and, maybe, how many concurrent users are to be expected and catered for.

If services are to be charged for, then details of the charging mechanism, together with the invoicing timescales and payment terms, will be included in the SLA or attached as an appendix (sometimes known as the tariff). The SLA will also include details on the method for making changes to the agreement as well as the time frame that the agreement covers. Contact details for both the IT Service Provider and the customers of the SLA should also be incorporated within the agreement.

The SLA for a service should be based on agreed targets that are both realistic and achievable. In order to deliver these realistic and achievable targets, the

IT Service Provider needs to ensure that all the components that make up the service can be delivered in terms of agreed performance, availability and other appropriate criteria. The components that make up the service may be provided by internal areas or may be sourced externally. By ensuring that the internal and external areas deliver their parts of the service as agreed, the IT Service Provider is able to agree an SLA with the business areas that includes levels of service that can actually be delivered.

The agreements required to underpin the SLA are OLAs for internal areas and UCs for external areas. With these in place, the IT Service Provider is in a position to deliver the agreed level of service rather than some aspirational level of service. Both OLAs and UCs should be negotiated and agreed prior to the final commitment to deliver the SLA.

Operational Level Agreements
Operational Level Agreements (OLAs) are drawn up between the IT Service Provider and internal areas. Having OLAs in place, covering aspects of the service in terms of performance and availability of components, gives the IT Service Provider confidence that the overall service can be delivered and allows them to enter into an SLA.

OPERATIONAL LEVEL AGREEMENT (OLA)

An agreement between an IT Service Provider and another part of the same organisation. An OLA supports the IT Service Provider's delivery of IT Services to the customers. The OLA defines the goods or services to be provided and the responsibilities of both parties. For example, there could be an Operational Level Agreement:

- between the IT Service Provider and a procurement department to obtain in agreed times;
- between the Service Desk and a support group to provide Incident resolution in agreed times.

Technical language may be included in OLAs, but they must remain understandable and be able to be linked to the appropriate SLAs. Legal language is not appropriate for OLAs because these are internal agreements and there would be no recourse to the law during disputes.

Underpinning Contracts
Underpinning Contracts (UCs) are drawn up between the IT Service Provider and external organisations or third parties. Having UCs in place, along with OLAs covering aspects of the service in terms of performance and availability of components, gives the IT Service Provider confidence that the overall service can be delivered and allows them to enter into an SLA.

UNDERPINNING CONTRACT (UC)

A contract between an IT Service Provider and a third party. The third party provides goods or services that support delivery of an IT Service to a customer. The Underpinning Contract defines targets and responsibilities that are required to meet agreed Service Level Targets in a Service Level Agreement.

The necessary legal language and protections will be used and built into UCs because the IT Service Provider is dealing with third parties external to the organisation. It is important to ensure that all UCs continue to support SLAs and to deliver parts of services or components that make up services that remain what the business areas require.

Service Level Manager

The Service Level Manager is the key role within Service Level Management. The Service Level Manager has the responsibility for managing the process. Service Owners also have an important role in ensuring that their services are delivered consistently to the agreed Service Levels. There is a close relationship between the Service Level Manager role and the Business Relationship Manager role. In many organisations, the two roles are combined. Business Relationship Management is in place to ensure that the IT Service Provider is meeting the aggregate business needs.

One issue that can arise for Service Level Managers and, in particular, Business Relationship Managers is that they are perceived within the IT Service Provider as being part of the business or acting in more of a business manner than in an IT Service Provider manner. This is not surprising because they are on the edge of the IT Service Provider facing the business. However, they also need to be in the midst of the IT Service Provider in order to know exactly what is going on with the provision of service. Staff within the IT Service Provider need to understand that one of the key elements of the Service Level Manager's role is to inform them about and advertise, across the IT Service Provider, the customer's perceptions and expectations in relation to the service received.

In order to succeed, Service Level Management is involved throughout the Service Lifecycle and interfaces with all other Service Management processes. SLM is particularly dependent on Service Portfolio Management and Service Catalogue Management because they are the sources of information on the services that SLM is to manage on a day-to-day basis.

DELIVERABLES

Main book references: SD 4.2.5.6, 4.2.5.7

There are a number of deliverables from Service Level Management. These include Service Reports and Service Improvement Plans, as well as conducting SLA Review meetings.

As soon as the SLA has been agreed and put in place, the reporting functionality must be available. Reporting timescales will have been agreed and it is often the case that exception reports will be required, meaning that there cannot be a delay in the provision of reports (i.e. reports may be required prior to the end of the first reporting period).

The SLA reporting requirements will have been discussed, negotiated and agreed as part of the Service Level Management process. The formats, timescales and reporting periods will have been set out in the SLA. The reporting should be aligned to the schedule of Service Review meetings. Again the frequency of Service Review meetings will have been discussed, agreed and documented within the SLA. The attendees of the Service Review meetings will need to have sight of the reports a few days prior to the meetings in order to be able to digest the information and to have time to undertake any necessary research.

Reporting should include all Service Level Targets for the period in question. Many organisations use a Service Level Monitoring (or SLAM) chart. This gives an easy to understand pictorial view of service performance using traffic light coding for performance against each Service Level Target. A service that has met the Service Level Target will be illustrated as green, ones that have failed the target will be red and those that have had issues, but have not breached the target thresholds, will be shown as amber. This traffic light style of reporting is often referred to as a RAG (Red Amber Green) report.

It is the role of Service Level Management to take the multiple feeds into the reporting process and convert them into clear, concise and meaningful reports. This can be a time-consuming activity, and sufficient time should be allowed to enable this compilation to take place. These multiple feeds into the process will come from internal suppliers reporting on OLAs, from external third-party suppliers reporting on UCs, from the Service Desk, Change Management, Availability Management, Capacity Management, Problem Management, Configuration Management etc. Reports should be automated as far as is possible, but need to be analysed carefully before being sent to the customer. The Service Level Management reporting requirements for Service Desk, Change Management, Problem Management, Availability Management, Capacity Management etc. should be included in the tool selection criteria for these areas.

Regular SLA Review meetings are a crucial part of the Service Level Management process. They allow discussion of reports, performance and issues, and are the vehicle for developing the relationship between the IT Service Provider and its customers. In addition to reporting and issue management (which tends to be backward looking), there will be the need to discuss future changes as well as future plans for both the IT Service Provider and the customer. Meetings should be formally minuted with actions and their allocated timescales. The minutes and actions from the previous meeting should be reviewed.

The SLA Review meetings must pay particular attention to Service Level breaches in the relevant period together with discussions over preventing reoccurrence and mitigating activity. If the number of breaches is increasing, it may be appropriate to discuss whether the targets remain correct. This does not mean that failure to deliver on a particular target results in an easier target, but that the relevance of targets needs to be continually reviewed. Any changes proposed for Service Levels or Service Targets must take into account the implications for the underpinning OLAs and the third-party UCs with external suppliers.

Review meetings provide the opportunity to exchange information as well as developing the relationship. It may be that the business areas have identified a forthcoming period of high activity or a period of increased risk that might require, for example, a moratorium on change. One of the key aspects that will be discussed is Continual Service Improvement.

SERVICE IMPROVEMENT PLAN (SIP)

A formal plan to implement improvements to a Process or IT Service.

During Service Review meetings, service improvements will be identified, discussed, costed and agreed, along with timescales and measures for success. These service improvements will be incorporated into the SIP and also the Service Quality Plan as part of the Continual Improvement stage of the Service Lifecycle.

Progress with SIP actions should be discussed and recorded during the regular Review meetings. It is also important to ascertain whether the SIP actions had the expected benefits and whether they were delivered at the agreed cost.

MONITORING SERVICE PERFORMANCE AGAINST SLAS

Main book references: SD 4.2.5.3, CSI 3.5

There is no point in including something in an SLA if it cannot be measured or monitored. The inability to measure or monitor will inevitably lead to disputes between the parties to the SLA. The same, of course, applies for OLAs and UCs. Monitoring capabilities should be in place when the SLA is agreed. It is the responsibility of Service Level Management to measure, monitor and report on SLA performance and to undertake and manage actions required to protect and improve that performance. Service Level Targets will be detailed within each SLA.

SERVICE LEVEL TARGET

A commitment that is documented in a Service Level Agreement. Service Level Targets are based on Service Level Requirements, and are needed to ensure that the IT Service Design is fit for purpose. Service Level Targets should be SMART, and are usually based on Key Performance Indicators.

Service Level Targets should only be agreed if they are specific, measurable, achievable, relevant and timely.

SMART

An acronym for helping to remember that targets in Service Level Agreements and project plans should be Specific, Measurable, Achievable, Relevant and Timely.

Service Level Management will work closely with its customers to discuss the delivery of service and how that delivery of service can be maintained and improved. They will also discuss and agree how the service will develop over time in the light of changing business requirements or changes in available technology. Service improvements need to be cost-effective and discussed and agreed with the business areas. The relationship between the IT Service Provider and the business areas will work best if it is open and constructive and not confrontational.

It is important to be able to monitor and measure service in the way that users see and receive the service. There may be a one second response time for an application in Head Office, while users in remote locations with slower network links are enduring five second response times. It needs to be understood that a balance is required. It will not be possible to monitor constantly the response time for each user and, ironically, when more monitoring tools are put in place, there is a risk that their existence leads to slower response times and a degraded service.

Response times are not always easy to monitor and measure. Where end-to-end response times are difficult to measure, organisations may include a statement in the SLA such as 'the service is designed in order to provide fast response times; however, if delays in excess of X seconds are experienced for longer than Y minutes, a call should be logged with the Service Desk'. There then should be a target for the number of such calls to the Service Desk in a reporting period.

It will make reporting easier and more straightforward if there is an Incident category of 'slow response' configured within the Service Desk tool. Trends in relation to slow responses will be picked up by Problem Management who will investigate and report back to Service Level Management and onwards to the customer via Service Level Management. Slow responses should be investigated immediately because it may be difficult to replicate the situation that existed in and across the infrastructure at a later date. Slow responses are often caused by a combination of factors coming together at a particular point in time.

While it is important that the service monitoring maps to the customer's perception of service, this is not always easy to do in practice. Users should be encouraged to advise the Service Desk if performance is not as it should be. However, it is important that the IT Service Provider and the business areas work together in order to ensure that the agreed performance levels are understood and advertised across the user community.

The reports issued by Service Level Management to customers should be in a format that is easy to read and understand. When visiting organisations, it is common to find very thick reports full of graphs and charts charting the performance of many things that make up the service. This is not what the customers want. They need to see clearly how the service has performed during the period. If there have been breaches, then these need to be detailed.

SERVICE REPORTING

The Process responsible for producing and delivering reports of achievement and trends against Service Levels. Service Reporting should agree the format, content and frequency of reports with customers.

Service Level Management is responsible for compiling and aggregating the reports, but they will rely on other areas for much of the information. The information may come from internal teams as well as external third parties. The requirement to provide the necessary information in an agreed format and in a timely manner will be incorporated in the relevant OLAs or UCs. This is another example of the IT Service Provider being able to deliver to the customer, in this case in terms of reporting, only if the SLA is underpinned by the OLAs and UCs.

Other areas of Service Management will also be important suppliers of reporting information to Service Level Management. These include the Service Desk who will provide details of Incident numbers and responses. It is important that the Service Desk tool is configured in such a way to allow the provision of information in the format agreed in the SLA. In reality, it will usually be the other way round with Service Level Management ascertaining what can be reported and how, and prior to discussing and agreeing the requirement with the customer. Capacity, Problem and Availability Management will also have important inputs to reporting. Where there are targets for the efficient handling of change and Requests for Change, the information should be made available to Service Level Management by Change Management using the reporting function of the Change Management tool.

KEY METRICS, CHALLENGES, CRITICAL SUCCESS FACTORS AND RISKS

Main book references: SD 4.2.7, 4.2.8, 4.2.9

A number of Key Performance Indicators (KPIs) and metrics can be used by Service Level Management in order to assess the performance of the process. As always, the process should be measured in terms that are meaningful from a business point of view. Service Level Management is in place to ensure that Service Level targets are identified, discussed, negotiated, agreed, documented, monitored and reported on. The metrics and KPIs should reflect this.

There are quite a few metrics that can be used to assess the effectiveness of the Service Level Management process in delivering services to the standards that have been agreed with the business. These include:

- the number of service breaches;
- the severity of service breaches;
- the frequency of service breaches;
- the number of services with up-to-date SLAs;
- the number of services with which SLA Review meetings have been conducted in the last quarter;
- the number of services with no SLA;
- the number of 'near misses' where service was nearly disrupted;
- the number of breaches caused by failures in the performance of OLAs;
- the number of breaches caused by failures in the performance of UCs;
- the number or percentage of SLA targets met;
- the number or percentage of SLAs where reports have been issued on time;
- the cost of monitoring SLA performance;
- the cost of time allocated to the development of new SLAs;
- the number of SLAs that prove to be defective and require renegotiation.

There may also be metrics centred on customer satisfaction surveys, such as the percentage improvement in customer satisfaction scores over the period. All these metrics provide a good insight into performance and any one of them could act as the catalyst for a Service Improvement Plan (SIP). The success of such a SIP would be measured by the future improvement in the metric. In some organisations, the Service Level Management area has its own budget for SIP activity: this is useful in encouraging a proactive approach to service improvements.

A softer indicator of how the Service Level Management process works is to view the attendee lists at Review Meetings. If very few business representatives appear or the attendees are always changing, this may be an indicator that something is not quite right, such as the business areas not being fully engaged in the process or in relationship building.

Some KPIs that can be used to assess and manage the quality of services delivered and also the number of services delivered are:

- percentage reduction in the number of SLA breaches;
- percentage reduction in the number of 'near misses' or threats to SLA targets;
- percentage reduction in SLA breaches attributable to failures to deliver under OLAs;
- percentage reduction in SLA breaches attributable to failures to deliver under UCs;
- percentage increase in customer satisfaction scores;
- percentage increase in the number of services covered by SLAs;
- percentage reduction in the cost of monitoring and reporting on SLAs;

- percentage increase in the speed of developing, negotiating and agreeing SLAs;
- percentage reduction in the number of SLAs that need to be renegotiated prior to their intended review date;
- percentage increase in the number of internal suppliers that are covered by OLAs.

The challenges that face Service Level Management include being to able to identify the correct people within the business areas to discuss and negotiate with. These should be the budget holders who have the authority to make decisions. Even when budget holders are involved at the negotiation stage, it is not always easy to keep them involved in the 'business as usual' aspects of the SLA. Often users represent the business areas at meetings and they tend to be more interested in response times and enhancements than the budget holder would be. Often there is a mismatch within the business areas where users complain about poor service without realising that they are receiving the service that the business has signed up to on the basis of budget available.

Timing of negotiations can also be a challenge. It is advisable to have OLAs and UCs in place prior to finalising the SLA. This can involve some juggling in order to keep everything coordinated. Another challenge can be the inability to accurately measure end-to-end response times and the risk of putting Service Targets in place that cannot be either measured or delivered. This can be overcome by agreeing draft targets that will be confirmed once the service and the measurement process are up and running.

There is also a risk that following lengthy negotiations on both sides, the finalised SLA will be left on a shelf 'to gather dust' both within the IT Service Provider and the Business areas. This should not be allowed to happen. The SLA is a living document and its contents should be advertised across the organisation.

Other risks include:

- the inability to measure performance leading to a lack of proactive improvements to service;
- the process being viewed as overly bureaucratic and cumbersome – this can be dispelled by demonstrating the service improvements that can be made by proactively managing SLAs;
- the lack of supporting information available from the Configuration Management System and the wider Service Knowledge Management System – this information is needed in order to map out all the components as well as internal and external suppliers that contribute to an end-to-end service.

The key Critical Success Factors for the Service Level Management process are:

- managing the overall quality of services required by customers;
- delivering the services in accordance with the agreements at the agreed price;
- managing and developing the relationship with the business areas and their users.

THE CONTENTS OF OLAS, SLAS AND REVIEW MEETINGS

Main book references: SD 4.2.5.5, 4.2.5.8, Appendix F

Operational Level Agreements

Not every Operational Level Agreement (OLA) will contain all of the sections listed below; however, all of the areas need to be taken into consideration when drawing up an OLA. Pragmatically, it would be a good idea to include all the areas in a first draft to ensure nothing is missed and then remove those areas that are not relevant for the particular OLA under construction.

Areas to consider

- **Introduction** to include:

    o Parties to the Agreement

    o Signatories

    o Start date

    o Expiry date

    o Brief description of the service

    o Review details and dates (such as quarterly or annually)

    o Allowance for minor changes to be agreed during the course of the OLA subject to the agreement of all parties and compliance with the Change Management process.

- **Details of previous alterations or amendments to the OLA.**

- **Support Service description:** To include a full description of the Support Service being provided.

- **Scope of the OLA:** To clearly set out what is included and is in scope, and what is excluded and is out of scope.

- **Service Hours:** When is the service available.

SERVICE HOURS

An agreed time period when a particular IT Service should be available. For example, 'Monday to Friday 8 a.m. to 5 p.m. except public holidays'. Service hours should be defined in a Service Level Agreement.

- **Service Targets:** Detail of all the agreed targets for the provision of the service together with the reporting mechanism, reviewing process and frequency.

- **Contact points:** Details of who should be contacted in what circumstances – this relates to all parties to the OLA.

- **Escalation:** What should be escalated, to whom, when and how.

- **Support of Service Desk:** How quickly the internal area should respond to Service Desk calls – there will be targets agreed for responding to and resolving Incidents referred by way of functional escalation by the Service Desk.

- **Support of Problem Management:** Similar to Incident Management – there will be targets agreed for responding to and resolving Problems referred by way of functional escalation by Problem Management.

- **Configuration Management:** Details of who is responsible for updating Configuration Management information and for ensuring that the applicable Configuration Management information is managed.

- **Change Management:** Details of targets and responsibilities for the raising, progressing and implementation of change.

- **Release Management:** Details of targets and responsibilities for the progressing and implementation of releases.

- **Access Management:** Details of who can have access, when they can have access, what they can have access to and how access is granted.

- **Information Security Management:** Details concerning responsibilities and targets in relation to the organisation's Security policy and the Information Security Management process.

- **Service Level Management:** Details of responsibilities on reporting and reviewing the service will be detailed in the Service Targets sections – this section in the body of the OLA will include any other responsibilities to Service Level Management and the Service Level Management process.

- **Supplier Management:** Details of the requirement for the involvement of the internal area in Supplier Management activity – this is likely to focus on providing technical input and assessment in relation to discussions with suppliers.

- **Capacity Management:** Responsibilities for supporting Capacity Management in relation to the use of the capabilities and resources within the internal area to provide technical input.

- **Financial Management:** To comply with all appropriate Financial governance frameworks.

- **Availability Management:** Details of the responsibilities for making sure that all components within the remit of the internal area signing up to the OLA are supported and managed in such a manner as to meet all the service availability targets as well as the component availability targets.

- **Service Continuity Management:** All components under the control of the internal support area that has signed up to the OLA must be managed in order to ensure that they support the organisation's Service Continuity process and have up-to-date and tested recovery plans – they will also need to provide input to the technical assessment of risk.

- **Provision of Information:** This area covers the maintenance and provision of relevant information in relation to the internal area covered by the OLA.

- **Glossary:** Lists anything that needs explaining – while OLAs can contain technical information, this should be at a level that can be easily understood by those managing and signing the OLA.

- **Amendment sheet:** A record of all agreed amendments together with details, dates and signatories.

- **Version control:** A complete document history for the OLA.

Service Level Agreements

Not every Service Level Agreement (SLA) will contain all of the sections listed below; however, all of the areas need to be taken into consideration when drawing up an SLA. Pragmatically, it would be a good idea to include all the areas in a first draft to ensure nothing is missed and then remove those areas that are not relevant for the particular SLA under construction.

Areas to consider

- **Introduction** to include:

  - Parties to the Agreement
  - Signatories
  - Start date
  - Expiry date
  - Brief description of the service
  - Review details and dates (such as quarterly or annually)
  - Allowance for minor changes to be agreed during the course of the SLA subject to the agreement of all parties and compliance with the Change Management process.

- **Details of previous alterations or amendments to the SLA.**

- **Service description:** To include a full description of the Service being provided including all deliverables and the important functionality – information on the service's priority to the business should also be included here.

- **Scope of the SLA:** To clearly set out what is included and in scope, and what is excluded and out of scope.

- **Service Hours:** Details when the service is available – this section should be quite specific (e.g. it will include details of public holidays and their impact on the service). The aim is to ensure that there is a common understanding of exactly when the service is going to be available throughout the period of the SLA. If agreed maintenance slots impact on the service hours, this information will be detailed here.

- **Service Availability:** To include the target availability levels for the service – these are normally expressed as percentages. It may be that details of the availability of key components and of the service overall are included here. Details of exactly how the availability of the service is to be derived and calculated should be included.

- **Reliability:** Details the number of service breaks allowed in a period – this is an important target, particularly when viewed in association with the availability target. Availability targets alone can be misleading about the robustness of a service, for example if there is an availability target of 95 per cent for a service provided 10 hours per day, one 30 minute outage gives 95 per cent availability for the day. However, two 15 minute outages, three 10 minute outages or six 5 minutes outages also give the same availability figure, but as the outages increase in number the impact on users tends to be greater and they lose faith in a service. Reliability targets may be phrased as number of breaches or as Mean Time Between Failures (MTBF) or Mean Time Between Service Incidents (MTBSI).

- **Support and Support Hours:** Details of how to contact the Service Desk, together with information on when the Service Desk is available and what to do outside the Service Desk's operating hours. Incident handling and response time targets will also be included in this section. There may also be details of the process for requesting an extension to the hours of support.

SUPPORT HOURS

The times or hours when support is available to the users. Typically these are the hours when the Service Desk is available. Support hours should be defined in a Service Level Agreement, and may be different from service hours. For example, service hours may be 24 hours a day, but support hours may be 7 a.m. to 7 p.m.

- **Contact points:** Details of who should be contacted in what circumstances – this relates to all parties to the SLA.

- **Escalation:** What should be escalated, to whom, when and how.

- **Service Performance:** Details of the expected response times – this should take into account the likely throughput levels.

- **Batch turnaround time:** Where a batch process has to run, information on when the batch should complete and the cut-off time to be part of the batch needs to be detailed.

- **Printing:** Any relevant printing details or deadlines.

- **Access Management:** Details of who can have access, when they can have access, what they can have access to and how access is granted.

- **Functionality:** Information on the minimum functionality to be provided.

- **Change Management:** A high-level overview of the organisation's Change Management process that is to be adhered to.

- **Service Continuity:** Details of continuity arrangements together with information on alternative sites and the testing programme.

- **Security:** Reference to the organisation's security policy and its requirements.

- **Responsibilities:** Details of the responsibilities of all the parties to the SLA.

- **Charging:** If appropriate, the charging details will appear here, including the tariff, charging period, invoicing requirements and payment terms. If there are penalty clauses or credit clauses, these should also appear here.

- **Service Reporting:** Details the frequency and content of reports together with the agreed distribution list.

- **Service Reviews:** The timetable of Service Reviews will be set out, sometimes with details of the agenda items that must be covered.

- **Glossary:** Lists anything within the body of the SLA that requires further explanation – this should be minimal because the SLA should be written in clear, concise, unambiguous business language.

- **Amendment sheet:** A record of all agreed amendments together with details, dates and signatories.

- **Version control:** A complete document history for the SLA.

Review Meetings

The following items should be included on the agenda:

- Attendees

- Apologies

- SLA performance against targets

- SLA reports

- Issues

- Disputes

- Outstanding Incidents and Problems

- Forthcoming changes

- Continual Service Improvement activity

- Any information useful to other parties for the forthcoming period

- Any other business

- Date of the next meeting

THE INTERFACE WITH OTHER PROCESSES AND FUNCTIONS

Main book references: SD 4.2.5 up to 4.2.5.1, Figure 4.5, 4.2.5.4, 4.2.5.8, 4.2.5.9, 4.2.6

Service Level Management acts as the focal point within the IT Service Provider for service issues, so it has many interfaces with other processes and areas.

There have to be strong links with the business areas, internal support teams, infrastructure areas and suppliers.

Service Level Management has interfaces to and depends on all other Service Management processes. Some of these relationships are stronger than others. The performance of Service Level Management would be less than optimal if any of the other Service Management processes were not fully implemented and operating effectively.

The following lists the key relationships for Service Level Management.

- **Service Portfolio Management:** Changes in the Service Portfolio will trigger Service Level Management activity. It is important that there are strong links between Service Portfolio Management and Service Level Management in order to ensure that there is a shared view and understanding of the services that are being delivered now and those that will be delivered in the future. Service Level Management assists Service Portfolio Management by contributing up-to-date information to the Service Portfolio and in particular to the Service Catalogue.

- **Service Catalogue Management:** One of the key mechanisms for building up trust and understanding with business areas is the use of the Service Catalogue and, in particular, the Business Service Catalogue part of the Service Catalogue. Information in the Business Service Catalogue enables Service Level Management to gain a greater understanding of the business processes that depend on the services they manage. This allows them to become more proactive in marketing services to business areas.

- **Change Management:** The ability to maintain service levels is very much dependent on there being an effective Change Management in place. Poorly planned or badly managed changes cause disruptions to services leading to an inability to reach Service Level Targets. Forward Schedule of Change information will be important to Service Level Management particularly when discussing plans for the forthcoming period with customers. Additionally, all SLAs, OLAs and UCs must be kept up to date and should be subject to Change Management Control.

- **Configuration Management:** The existence of a well-maintained and effective Configuration Management System will reduce the risks of changes and release failures caused by a lack of understanding of how the infrastructure fits together. With fewer failures, Service Level targets are more likely to be met. Additionally, all SLAs, OLAs and UCs should be recorded as Configuration Items within the Configuration Management System. If this is the case, it will be easier to assess the impact of changes to the agreements or contracts in a controlled manner.

- **Release Management:** This is similar to Change Management in that failed or delayed releases will have an adverse impact on the delivery of service. These failures or delays will in turn lead to threats or breaches to Service Level Targets. Robust and effective Release Management minimises service disruptions.

- **Request Fulfilment:** Complaints and compliments are received on a day-to-day basis by the Service Desk. It is often the Request Fulfilment process that progresses these complaints and compliments. Having an up-to-date understanding of the issues causing complaints or triggering compliments is very useful for Service Level Management in their discussions with business areas.

- **Service Desk and Incident Management:** The Service Desk and Incident Management processes are concerned with restoring service as quickly as possible in order to protect Service Level Targets. The Service Desk is very important to Service Level Management because it is the area that has the most user contact. It also provides a large input to the Service Level Management reporting process.

- **Problem Management:** Problem Management is involved both reactively and proactively in resolving problems that threaten or impinge on the delivery of service. Problem Management contributes to the Service Level Management reporting process. The proactive side of Problem Management is particularly important to Service Level Management when drawing up and executing Service Improvement Plans.

- **Availability Management:** Availability Management will report to Service Level Management on performance as well as highlighting issues and opportunities. These opportunities may have arisen due to the introduction of new technology. Availability Management is also able to give Service Level Management advice, information and support in discussions with business areas and suppliers. Availability Management also produces the Projected Service Outage document that will be very useful to Service Level Management in discussions about future plans with business areas.

- **Service Continuity Management:** Service Continuity Management will conduct Business Impact Analysis, which will provide information on the impact, priority, risk and the number of users using each service. This is very useful to Service Level Management because it enables them to understand the relative priorities to the business areas of the services being delivered.

- **Capacity Management:** Capacity Management will report to Service Level Management on performance as well as highlighting issues and opportunities. These opportunities may have arisen due to the introduction of new options or methods for delivering capacity. Capacity Management is also able to provide Service Level Management with advice, information and support in discussions with business areas and suppliers.

10 DEMAND MANAGEMENT

INTRODUCTION

Demand Management plays an important role within Service Management. Effective Demand Management prevents unnecessary expenditure on capacity. It also minimises reductions in the level of service caused by fluctuations in workload or throughput.

DEMAND MANAGEMENT

Demand Management covers Activities that understand and influence customer demand for Services and the provision of capacity to meet these demands. At a strategic level Demand Management can involve analysis of Patterns of Business Activity and user profile. At a tactical level it can involve use of Differential Charging to encourage customers to use IT Services at less busy times.

If demand is not properly managed it becomes a potential risk for an organisation. The risk centres on uncertainty around the level of demand, which tends to lead to excess capacity being put in place. Excess capacity is not an effective use of resources because it produces cost without creating value. Business areas will not be keen on paying for excess capacity if it does not generate value for them.

IT Service Providers should be providing just enough capacity for services to meet their agreed service levels. The goal of Demand Management is to optimise the use of capacity by moving workload to less utilised resources and to less utilised times of the day, week, month etc. In this way, more efficient use is made of the resources because their utilisation is evened out over time rather than having to cater for peaks or troughs in workload. The purpose of Demand Management is to predict, understand and influence the demand from customers for services in order to support the provision and management of minimum capacity to meet these demands.

Effective Demand Management has the following benefit. Once the Demand Management process has predicted and understood fluctuations in demand and applied controls to limit peak demand, Capacity Management becomes more effective in planning capacity, reducing unnecessary expenditure and procuring resources more effectively. Resources can be procured more effectively because there is no panic buying and the organisation is in a position to fully research the market and the options for purchasing capacity. More effective planning, reductions in unnecessary expenditure and procurement of resources will lead to improved service levels. Improved service levels lead in turn to increased confidence from the business areas in the ability of the IT Service Provider to meet both present and future requirements.

The objectives of Demand Management are:

- to understand and predict the demand for services and the accompanying demand for IT resources;
- to encourage the use of services at non-peak times.

BASIC CONCEPTS

Main book reference: SS 5.5.1

The Demand Management process is required for two reasons:

- The demand for services is rarely constant. Demand is the source of work, such as the submission of a transaction or a web search. Demand comes from the business areas in relation to the services they receive. There will also be internal demand from within the IT Service Provider that needs to be catered for. Demand is also used to refer to the workload that is subsequently generated on IT resources by activities such as transactions or web searches. Network usage is an obvious example. Demand is not constant with peaks and troughs throughout each hour, day, month etc. Demand for some services may be seasonal. It is rare for there to be sufficient flexibility in the available IT resources in order to provide just enough capacity to meet the demand through all the peaks and troughs.

- There is an inherent risk with attempting to provide just the right amount of capacity. There is little margin for error especially because predicting demand can be an inexact science. The IT Service Provider will want to manage and minimise the risk of insufficient capacity at any point in time leading to degraded or interrupted service. There is a balance to be struck and it is the business areas who, properly informed by the IT Service Provider, will need to decide on the level of risk they are prepared to accept. They will often accept some spare capacity with the accompanying cost implications in order to reduce the risk to service. Where this is the case, the excess capacity does create value for the business because it provides a higher level of assurance.

Lack of capacity leads to degraded or interrupted service and also puts a limitation on the growth potential of the service in that the service cannot grow until extra capacity is made available. The use of forecasting and close liaison with the business areas through both Capacity Management and Service Level Management can reduce the uncertainties around demand, but they cannot be completely eradicated.

In order to predict the demand for services, Demand Management undertakes the production of user profiles and common service consumption profiles. User profiles are used to illustrate the characteristics of the users of a particular service. Common service consumption profiles are intended to highlight which business activities have similar consumption patterns. They are created by characterising and codifying business activities into specific and recognisable patterns in order to ascertain which have common consumption profiles. The adoption of user profiles and common service consumption profiles makes it easier for the IT Service Provider to match the services and resources to the needs of each user profile that has been identified. The end result is that value is increased as both poor service and costs are minimised.

One of the main issues for Demand Management is that services cannot be stock-piled in anticipation of future demand. A steel manufacturer, for example, can stockpile output to ensure demand can be met in the future. However, services are not like goods and they cannot be manufactured or assembled in advance. For services, it is consumption that produces demand and it is production that consumes demand in a manner that is highly synchronised. This is illustrated in Figure 10.1.

Figure 10.1 Relationship between consumption, demand and production
(Source: OGC ITIL Service Strategy ISBN 978-0-113310-45-6)

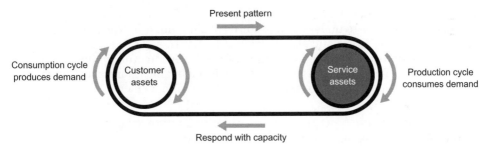

The diagram shows the synchronous production and consumption. The production of services can only occur when demand is present and it is that same demand that consumes the production.

Techniques such as Differential Charging or off-peak charging can be used to influence the arrival of demand. Another approach is to produce differentiated service levels. There are, if necessary, more draconian steps that can be taken, such as restricting the number of concurrent users. Throttling demand in such a fashion should only really be done as a last resort because it is not user-friendly and will lead to a strained relationship with the user community.

DIFFERENTIAL CHARGING

A technique that is used to support Demand Management by charging different amounts for the same IT Service Function at different times.

In order to instigate Differential Charging, the IT Service Provider must first persuade the business areas that this is in their best interests. The aim is to avoid expenditure on capacity that would not always be used. This is done by attempting to influence demand in such a way as to reduce peak workloads and protect service from degradation or interruption. Differential Charging involves increasing the price for units of work at peak times and/or reducing the price for units of work at off-peak times.

Differential Charging and differentiated service levels have their merits, but the underlying issue that demand cannot do anything other than use capacity at the point in time it is demanded remains. Services cannot be produced prior to the demand appearing.

ACTIVITY-BASED DEMAND MANAGEMENT AND BUSINESS ACTIVITY PATTERNS

Main book references: SS 5.5.2, 5.5.3, Figure 5.2.3

The workload that creates demand originates from the business processes. There is a clear link between the business processes and the consumption of IT resources experienced by the IT Service Provider. In order to understand the demand that the business processes create, Patterns of Business Activity are identified.

Figure 10.2 shows how business activity patterns influence patterns of demand for services. In order to understand patterns of demand, it is crucial to under-stand the business areas and exactly what it is that they do. A good and close working relationship is needed with the business areas in order to understand their plans for the future. They will have produced business forecasts that will be vital input to Capacity Management and Demand Management.

Figure 10.2 Business activity patterns influence demand for service
(Source: OGC ITIL Service Strategy ISBN 978-0-113310-45-6)

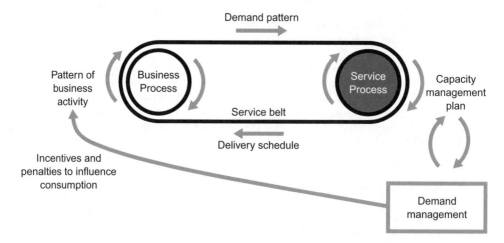

The production and sharing of business plans and forecasts will enable the IT Service Provider to predict and anticipate the impact on IT resources. This allows the identification of IT resources that will need to be upgraded, replaced or added to in order to meet the future demand. In this way, expenditure on new IT resources or upgrading existing IT resources can be done in a cost-effective manner without the need for panic buying.

Service Level Management and Business Relationship Management are very useful areas to seek information on the activities of the business areas. There has to be a real understanding of what the business processes are, why they occur and what happens when they occur. Figure 10.3 shows an example of activity-based Demand Management.

Figure 10.3 An example of activity-based Demand Management (Source: OGC ITIL Service Strategy ISBN 978-0-113310-45-6)

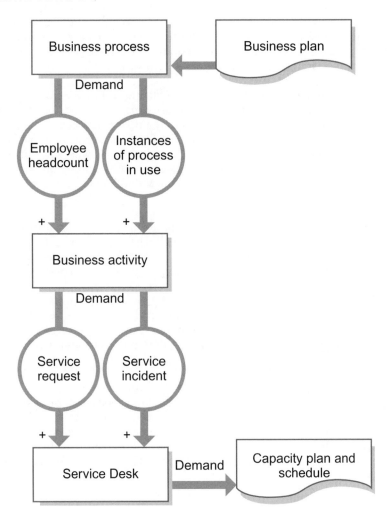

The activity of the business area is shown as being business processes conducted by a number of users. If each user conducts the same number of transactions, for example, the addition of new users can quickly be translated into an increased demand. Future demand can be predicted by understanding the relationship between the users and the business processes that they use.

The Service Desk is an ideal area to visualise demand where the drivers for business demand can usually be easily understood and the workload predicted. Service Desk staffing will respond to demand fluctuation brought about by the business activities. The working hours of the business will be known and there will be peaks and troughs during these working hours.

The Service Desk will be aware of the profile of business activity on an hourly, daily, weekly, monthly and yearly basis. As well as the predictable peaks and troughs of the profile, there will be other times when demand fluctuations can be anticipated, for example, after a major release. Staffing levels can be adjusted accordingly in order to match the peaks and troughs of demand. There should, however, be some contingency in place for peaks or troughs of demand that cannot be anticipated (such as a service failure). Activity-based Demand Management focuses on visualising the customer's business processes and plans in terms of demand for services and reacting accordingly.

The IT Service Provider is able to manage the demand that the business processes create by understanding the business processes and their impact on IT resources. A particular business process may impact on a large number of IT components and across a large part of the IT infrastructure. It is important to understand the impact of the demand at all levels. The Service Catalogue is a useful tool in this area because it contains details of the components and infrastructure that underpin each service as well as the links between services and the business processes.

Where the business areas are planning to expand their activities or introduce new products, the likely levels of demand for IT Services will need to be predicted. A demand model can be developed over time, so that changes in business activity can be quickly translated into the expected impact on IT resources.

If demand patterns are known, then Service Design is in a position to take them into account when designing new or upgraded services. On a day-to-day basis, Service Operation will react to shifts in demand. Financial Management will be able to work on the possibilities of motivating demand once demand patterns are fully understood.

Future demand levels can be predicted by understanding business activities and how they generate demand for services. It is the business users, processes and applications that create Patterns of Business Activity. The Patterns of Business Activity for a particular business area very much define and illustrate what that business area is all about. It is crucial to understand Patterns of Business Activity because they generate the service demand and income for the IT Service Provider.

THE INTERFACE TO THE SERVICE PORTFOLIO

Main book reference: SS 5.5.2

The Service Portfolio contains details of all services in the Service Pipeline, Service Catalogue and Retired Services. It is important to understand the demand for those services in operation and those services that are to be transitioned into operation (i.e. those in the Service Pipeline and those in the Service Catalogue).

Service Design is able to take into account patterns of demand as services are being designed. The patterns of likely demand will be reconfirmed as the services are developed and prior to transition into the live environment. Gaining an understanding of potential future business demand involves forging and maintaining a close relationship with the business areas and, in particular, with their planning and forecasting functions.

The Service Catalogue is used to examine the impact of changes in the patterns of demand on all services in operation or ready for operation. Anticipated alterations in the patterns of demand can be assessed in terms of potential and likely impact on components and the infrastructure by reference to the Service Catalogue. This is because the Service Catalogue contains details of the components and infrastructure that underpin each service as well as the links between services and the business processes.

It is not just the impact on live services that should be considered where changes in the patterns of demand are identified. The Service Pipeline will contain details of services that are being developed. The rationale and business cases for these new services may need to be revisited in the light of the changing patterns of demand.

Service Portfolio Management is concerned with ensuring that all services provide value and are delivered in a cost-effective manner. Investments in new capacity will be considered by Service Portfolio Management in response to changing Patterns of Business Activity. It may be that the changes in business activity trigger the requirement for new or revised services. A change in the pattern of business demand represents a change in the environment in which services are delivered and this change, like any other, should be considered in terms of its impact on the Service Portfolio.

MANAGING DEMAND FOR SERVICE

Main book references: SS 5.5.3, Table 5.8, Table 5.9

The Patterns of Business Activity should be identified and codified to allow analysis. This should be done for all business processes and across all services in order to obtain the aggregate picture. Each business process will be examined in order to understand its frequency, volume, location and duration. Additionally, there may be security or privacy requirements. Table 10.1 gives an example of the codification of business activity.

Table 10.1 Example of codifying Patterns of Business Activity (Source: OGC ITIL Service Strategy ISBN 978-0-113310-45-6)

PBA No. 45F Activities	Activity levels High	3	2	1	Low	N/A
Interact with customers remotely (frequency)			X			
Interact with customers on site (frequency)				X		
Archive or handle customer information			X			
Process sensitive information (privacy)						X
Generate confidential information						X
Provide technical support (frequency)		X				
Seek technical assistance				X		
Network bandwidth requirements		X				
Data storage requirements (volume)		X				
Tolerance for delay in service response			X			
Seasonal variations in activity				X		
Print documents and images			X			
Mailing of documents using third party systems			X			
Process transactions with wireless mobile device				X		
Email using wireless device					X	
Access work systems during domestic travel				X		
Access work systems during overseas travel					X	

Patterns of Business Activity should be placed under Change Control. This is because they can change over time due to changes in the business processes, staffing and in the general environment in which the business operates. Over time a number of coded Patterns of Business Activity will be built up. These can be compared for common characteristics that when identified may lead to efficiencies, driven through Demand Management, impacting in more than one area.

Patterns of Business Activity can often be associated with a small number of defined user profiles. User profiles are centred on roles and responsibilities for individuals and on functions and operations for processes and applications. Increasing automation means that it is not only people that trigger the use of processes. User profiles should be put in place no matter how the business processes are triggered. The use of user profiles allows demand planning to take place. For example, when a new member of staff is recruited, their future demands on the Service Desk are anticipated based on the general user profile for staff in that area without the need to consider them individually.

Table 10.2 shows that each user profile can be linked to one or more Patterns of Business Activity.

Table 10.2 Example of user profiles matched with Patterns of Business Activity
(Source: OGC ITIL Service Strategy ISBN 978-0-113310-45-6)

User profile	Applicable Pattern of Business Activity (PBA)	PBA code
Senior executive (UP1)	Moderate travel – domestic and overseas; highly sensitive information; zero latency on Service Requests; high need for technical assistance; need to be highly available to the business	45F 45A 35D
Highly mobile executive (UP2)	Extensive travel – domestic and overseas; sensitive information; low latency on Service Requests; moderate need for technical assistance; high customer contact; need to be highly available to customers	45A 35D 22A
Office-based staff (UP3)	Office-based administrative staff; low travel – domestic; medium latency on Service Requests; low need for technical assistance; full-featured desktop needs; moderate customer contact; high volume of paperwork; need to be highly productive during work hours	22A 14B 3A
Payment processing system (UP4)	Business system; high volume; transaction-based; high security needs; low latency on Service Requests; low seasonal variation; mailing of documents by postal service; automatic customer notification; under regulatory compliance; need for low unit costs; need to be highly secure and transparent (audit control)	12F

(Continued)

Table 10.2 *(Continued)*

User profile	Applicable Pattern of Business Activity (PBA)	PBA code
Customer assistance process (UP5)	Business process; moderate volume; transaction-based; moderate security needs; very low latency on service requests; medium seasonal variation; mailing of replacement parts by express; automatic customer notification; need to be highly responsive to customers	24G 10G

Linking user profiles with Patterns of Business Activity lets the IT Service Provider understand and then manage demand from the business areas more easily and accurately. User profiles relate to Patterns of Business Activity that are repeated and correlated, and so are predictable. Change Control should apply to user profiles for the same reasons that Patterns of Business Activity are placed there.

User profiles are also very useful tools for the business areas. Their creation often allows possible efficiencies to be identified in the business processes. They enable business areas to identify more readily where and why they incur cost by way of the use of services. Linking together Patterns of Business Activity with user profiles enables those responsible for the services provided by the IT Service Provider to predict and respond to changing levels of demand. In this way degraded performance and unnecessary expenditure on capacity is minimised and value for both customers and the IT Service Provider is enhanced.

11 SUPPLIER MANAGEMENT

INTRODUCTION

This chapter covers the use of the Supplier Management process together with the interfaces and dependencies of the process. The Supplier Management process makes sure that all suppliers, as well as the services they provide, are managed in such a way to ensure that Service Targets are met.

SUPPLIER

A third party responsible for supplying goods or services that are required to deliver IT Services. Examples of Supplier include commodity hardware and software vendors, network and telecom providers and outsourcing organisations.

Very few IT services are delivered totally 'in-house', for example IT Service Providers will often rely on externally sourced software or third-party network links in order to deliver a service. Hardware maintenance is another area that is often provided by an external supplier.

SUPPLIER MANAGEMENT

The Process responsible for ensuring that all contracts with Suppliers support the needs of the business, and that all Suppliers meet their contractual commitments.

In many aspects, the external suppliers are managed in a similar way to internal suppliers who provide part of a particular service. The key difference is that while internal suppliers are managed via Operational Level Agreements, external suppliers are managed via Contracts that aim to underpin the service. These contracts contain all the necessary legal safeguards.

CONTRACT

A legally binding agreement between two or more parties.

The complexity of networks, for example, combined with the economies of scale enjoyed by network providers, leads to many organisations purchasing these resources from external service providers who are third parties. There are also large initial set-up costs for network provision (especially where sites are geographically spread) that act as a barrier to organisations providing them in-house. This also lets organisations concentrate on their core services.

THIRD PARTY

A person, group or business that is not part of the Service Level Agreement for an IT Service, but is required to ensure successful delivery of that IT Service. Examples of third parties include a software supplier, a hardware maintenance company or a facilities department. Requirements for third parties are typically specified in Underpinning Contracts or Operational Level Agreements.

EXTERNAL SERVICE PROVIDER

An IT Service Provider that is part of a different organisation to its customer. An IT Service Provider may have both internal customers and external customers.

The Supplier Management process is wider than contract negotiation and ongoing contract management. It needs to ensure that the organisation is getting good value for money from suppliers. Relationships need to be built and managed with suppliers. The relationship with a supplier should not merely be seen as a static situation. The relationship will change and mature over time. Supplier relationships will evolve as the commercial environment changes and as the technical options increase.

It is important that a formal contract is negotiated, agreed and put in place where external third-party suppliers are being used. This contract should contain responsibilities that are clearly defined and documented along with measurable targets. The contract should then be managed throughout its lifecycle to termination. The contract lifecycle, therefore, will cover the activities from the identification of business need, through identification, negotiation, agreement and documentation of the contract and operation, to renewal or termination.

Contracts should be effective and clearly understood by both sides. It would be counter-productive for an organisation to drive down price to such a level that the supplier cannot continue to deliver or is forced into a position where they have no alternative other than to instigate fees for variations in the contract that would normally be seen as business as usual.

Organisations will want to ensure that they obtain value for money from their suppliers and that the suppliers adhere to the contracts by delivering in accordance with the agreed targets. This is the role of Supplier Management. Continual Service Improvement needs to be built into the customer–supplier relationship and this relationship should be the starting point for increasing service quality and value for money.

PURPOSE, GOAL AND OBJECTIVES

Main book reference: SD 4.7.1

The purpose of Supplier Management is to ensure suppliers meet their targets and to obtain value for money.

The goal of the Supplier Management process is to manage suppliers and the services they supply, to provide seamless quality of IT Service to the business, ensuring value for money is obtained.

Supplier Management manages suppliers in order to obtain the best possible value for the organisation. Some services may be delivered using only internal resources, but increasingly the delivery of IT Services has become dependent on a blend of internal and external suppliers. Some services are purchased in their entirety from third parties. Supplier Management manages the relationships with these third parties.

Suppliers need to be managed throughout the lifecycle of the relationship between an organisation and the supplier. Suppliers, and therefore Supplier Management, must be involved through each stage of the Service Lifecycle by discussing options and possibilities in Service Strategy and Design, by supporting their products in Service Transition and Service Operation, and by providing ongoing Continual Service Improvement.

Many mature customer–supplier relationships have a 'working with partners' focus. Long-term relationships are fostered and increasingly mutual goals allow risks and rewards to be shared. Use of partnerships and value networks is often a key part of the delivery of complex services, and the relationships within the partnerships and value networks need to be managed.

PARTNERSHIP

A relationship between two organisations that involves closely working together for common goals or mutual benefit. The IT Service Provider should have a Partnership with the Business and with Third Parties who are critical to the delivery of IT Services.

SUPPLY CHAIN

A Supply Chain is made up of the activities in a Value Chain that are carried out by Suppliers. A Supply Chain typically involves multiple Suppliers, each adding value to the product or service.

Although supplier relationships may become more like partnerships with mutual benefits, there remains a need to ensure that the relationships are structured and managed via the contracts. The supplier needs to deliver in accordance with the terms and conditions of the contract and to meet the delivery targets.

The key objectives of Supplier Management are:

- to manage relationships with Suppliers both day to day and strategically;
- to manage the performance of Suppliers ensuring that performance is in accordance with the terms of the contract and that they deliver good value for money;
- to identify, negotiate and agree contracts with Suppliers and then to manage the contracts throughout their lifecycle;
- to ensure that the UCs agreed with suppliers are aligned to the needs of the business – this involves working with Service Level Management to ensure that the business needs enshrined in the Service Level Requirements and SLAs are reflected in the targets set and agreed in the UCs;
- to develop, populate and maintain a Supplier and Contract Database;
- to develop and maintain a supplier policy.

THE SCOPE OF THE PROCESS

Main book reference: SD 4.7.2

The scope of Supplier Management covers the management of all the suppliers and contracts required to support the delivery of the IT Services provided by the IT Service Provider. The scope is all suppliers and a process needs to be in place to cover it. However, it is recognised that suppliers come in different shapes and sizes, and that some will be more important than others. Therefore the processes need to be able to recognise and adjust to the significance of a particular supplier.

The significance of a supplier will be determined by the business criticality of the service to which they are contributing. There will be other factors that influence supplier significance, such as the availability or otherwise of alternative suppliers and whether or not a supplier provides a contribution to several services within an organisation. The more important the supplier, the more need for proactive management, especially where they support a key service delivered by the IT Service Provider.

The amount of time and effort put into managing a particular supplier should be proportional to the contribution that the particular supplier makes to business value. Suppliers that make a considerable contribution to business value are likely to be involved in developing and maybe delivering some part of business strategy. Business areas will require far less involvement with suppliers whose contribution to business value is not significant, and such relationships are more likely to be managed at an operational level.

It is important to maintain the drive for the delivery of value for money from suppliers. In order to highlight this, each supplier should have an owner within Supplier Management and the IT Service Provider. Figure 11.1 shows how this may operate with individuals owning one or more supplier relationships.

Figure 11.1 Supplier ownership (Source: OGC ITIL Service Design ISBN 978-0-113310-47-0)

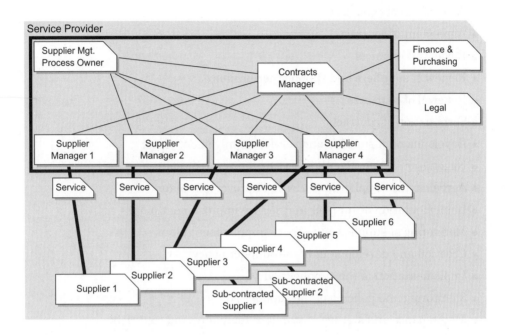

In the diagram, the Supplier Managers are the owners of the supplier relationships.

The diagram also shows a number of roles within Supplier Management (i.e. Supplier Manager, Supplier Management Process Owner and Contracts Manager). These roles are important in order to ensure that relationships with suppliers are consistent and that performance is monitored. For smaller organisations, these roles will be combined. The diagram also indicates the input of the organisation's Finance and Purchasing and Legal controls that will provide a governance framework of corporate guidelines and standards.

The following subprocesses should be included in the Supplier Management process:

- Risk assessment of suppliers
- Risk assessment of contracts
- Categorisation of suppliers (e.g. tactical or strategic)
- Categorisation of contracts
- Evaluation of suppliers
- Evaluation of contracts
- Selection of suppliers
- Selection of contracts

113

- Drawing up of contracts (often iterative with the contracts developing as negotiations take place)
- Negotiation of contracts
- Agreement of contracts
- Review of contracts
- Review of suppliers and supplier performance
- Renewal of contracts
- Termination of contracts
- Development of supplier and service improvement plans
- Negotiation of supplier and service improvement plans
- Agreement of supplier and service improvement plans
- Implementation of supplier and service improvement plans
- Monitoring of supplier and service improvement plans
- Creation and development of the supplier policy
- Implementation of the supplier policy
- Monitoring and policing of the supplier policy
- Maintenance and storage of standard templates and contracts
- Design of Supplier and Contract Database
- Development of Supplier and Contract Database
- Population of Supplier and Contract Database
- Maintenance of Supplier and Contract Database

THE IMPORTANCE OF THE PROCESS TO THE SERVICE LIFECYCLE AND HOW IT GENERATES BUSINESS VALUE

Main book reference: SD 4.7.3

Supplier Management generates business value by obtaining value for money from all suppliers and contracts. Supplier Management is able to be certain that the parts of services provided by third parties are contributing properly to the meeting of business needs and requirements by doing this and by ensuring that all the contracts are properly aligned to the business needs of the organisation.

Supplier Management also contributes to the Service Lifecycle and adds business value by ensuring that all contracts and all suppliers adhere to the organisation's corporate requirements. This is particularly important in the areas of security and continuity.

The value Supplier Management contributes to the Service Lifecycle is not always immediate. There are benefits of building long-term relationships with key suppliers.

If a good relationship is in place, sometimes benefits may accrue when seeking help developing new services or maybe when managing major incidents that are not strictly covered by the terms of the contract. In order to develop the relationship, positive and proactive management is needed all the way through the lifecycle of a contract or of a supplier relationship. This involves monitoring and liaising with suppliers with the aim of identifying issues before they have an impact on service, as well as working together on continual service improvement.

In order to obtain value for money over the longer term, the organisation has to know what direction it is heading in, including what services it will offer in the future and how it will deliver them. To do this, the future business needs have to be understood and translated into potential new services. The organisation will then need to understand its own available resources and capabilities in relation to the potential new services and this allows the requirement for outside assistance to be understood. Once this is known, together with the risks of different levels of supplier involvement, the relationship with existing or potential suppliers can be directed and managed in such a way to derive future value for money.

PRINCIPLES AND BASIC CONCEPTS

Main book reference: SD 4.7.4

The Supplier Management process is in place to ensure that all contracts and all suppliers deliver value for money and that this value for money is maximised. This is done in a number of ways, but principally by managing contracts and suppliers to make sure the terms and conditions are adhered to and that targets are met. The targets within contracts negotiated with suppliers should reflect the business needs expressed in the Service Level Requirements and the Service Level Agreements.

Supplier Management activity must be dictated by the organisation's overall supplier strategy, which is derived in the Service Strategy phase of the Service Lifecycle. A high-level view of the Supplier Management process is shown in Figure 11.2.

The diagram shows the strategy and policy input, together with the cycle of process activity from evaluation of new suppliers and contracts through establishing contracts and monitoring contracts, to renewing or terminating contracts. The glue that sticks all of this together and stores and controls all the information is the Supplier and Contract Database, the use of which allows a consistent approach to be taken to all suppliers and contracts. The Supplier and Contract Database contains all the information required in order to conduct all the Supplier Management tasks. A Supplier and Contract Database needs to be in place and roles and responsibilities must be clearly defined in order for Supplier Management to be effective.

The information within the Supplier and Contract Database is provided by and supports all of the stages of the Service Lifecycle. Service Design will provide the information on supplier evaluation and supplier and contract selection together

Figure 11.2 Supplier Management process activities (Source: OGC ITIL Service Design ISBN 978-0-113310-47-0)

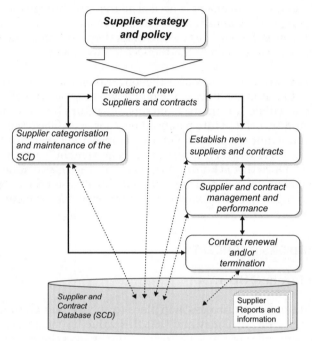

with details of supplier and contract categorisation. The maintenance activities undertaken in relation to the Supplier and Contract Database will also be defined and documented during Service Design. Service Transition will provide details of taking on a supplier and set up while Service Operation will be able to furnish the Supplier and Contract Database with up-to-date information on supplier and contract performance. Contract renewal and termination details will also come from Service Operation.

The Supplier and Contract Database should form part of an integrated Service Knowledge Management System or Configuration Management System with links between the supplier and contract details with all the Configuration Items involved. This will allow a holistic view to be taken of a particular supplier's contribution and importance to an organisation's service provision. Details of services purchased from suppliers will also be recorded in the Service Catalogue and the Service Portfolio.

Contracts should be negotiated so they are consistent with the needs of the business. This seems obvious, but in reality it is not always easy to translate a business wish into the necessary legal terms and conditions required by a contract. This is why the business needs are formulated and distilled into Service Level Requirements and then Service Level Agreements. The targets set out in supplier contracts will be in line with and contribute to the Service Level Targets allowing the third-party delivered portion of the overall service to provide what is expected and required.

Business needs change, so contracts with suppliers should be reviewed to ensure that they meet the revised needs. This review may necessitate the renegotiation or the termination of some contracts as well as the creation of new contracts with existing and new suppliers. It is not just business needs that may change and cause the contracts and suppliers to be reviewed in order to ensure that they are still delivering value for money: there may also be changes in technology, competition, legislation or market conditions.

Ensuring that value for money is maximised involves ongoing monitoring of existing as well as potential suppliers. Existing suppliers may have new products or new suppliers may have entered the market. Organisations may also review contracts with a particular supplier if they believe they are becoming too dependent on that supplier. Supplier Management is an iterative process and so the business value is generated both in the short term and in the long term.

ACTIVITIES, RELATIONSHIP TO THE SERVICE LIFECYCLE, AND EVALUATION OF NEW SUPPLIERS

Main book references: SD 4.7.5 up to 4.7.5.2, 4.7.5.3, 4.7.5.4, 4.7.5.5

The main activities of Supplier Management are:

- the initiation, development, documentation, implementation and management of a supplier policy;
- the initiation, development, implementation and management of a Supplier and Contract Database;
- the development, documentation and maintenance of standard terms and conditions to be included within contracts;
- the identification of business needs and the development and building of a business case;
- the evaluation, selection and procurement of new suppliers and contracts including the negotiation and agreement of contracts;
- the establishment of new suppliers and contracts;
- the categorisation of suppliers and contracts including risk assessment;
- the management of supplier and contract performance;
- the management and resolution of disputes;
- the renewal or termination of contracts.

The following paragraphs look at these in more detail.

The initiation, development, documentation, implementation and management of a supplier policy

The Supplier policy and strategy governs the Supplier Management process. The organisation's Supplier policy and strategy provides the framework for how the organisation will use external third-party suppliers and how the organisation will engage with these suppliers. The policy will include and cover the selection of suppliers and the ongoing management of relationships with suppliers. The supplier policy for government organisations is often dictated by legislation that clearly sets out what needs to be done, particularly around tendering.

The initiation, development, implementation and management of a Supplier and Contract Database

The Supplier and Contract Database allows Supplier Management to manage effectively all the relevant supplier and contract information. The Supplier and Contract Database contains information on all suppliers and contracts together with details of the goods and services provided by each supplier. A holistic view can be taken across all suppliers and across all services to see where an organisation is dependent on one or more suppliers.

The Supplier and Contract Database is used throughout the lifecycle of a contract or supplier relationship. Contact details including renewal and termination dates will be held along with up-to-date contact information. Depending on the importance and degree of the relationship with the supplier, the contact information may be quite detailed with a hierarchy of contacts within the supplier matched by Supplier Management responsibilities within the purchasing organisation.

The initiation, development and implementation of a Supplier and Contract Database should ideally be aligned to the development of the Configuration Management System. The Supplier and Contract Database should be part of both the Configuration Management System and the wider Service Knowledge Management System. This again allows a holistic view to be taken of a supplier's influence and importance across the infrastructure and services and allows risks to be highlighted and then managed. There will also be links between the information held in the Supplier and Contract Management Database and the information in the Service Portfolio and the Service Catalogue.

(The management of the Supplier Contract Database is covered in more detail in the next section: The use of Supplier Categorisation and maintenance of the Supplier and Contract Database.)

The development, documentation and maintenance of standard terms and conditions to be included within contracts

There are a number of areas that must be covered within a contract and a number of other areas that may be included. Contracts are usually drawn up with the main part containing all the necessary commercial and legal clauses together with attached schedules containing the service elements of the contract.

These service elements include:

- Description of Service and Scope of Service including functionality, availability, performance, security and technical interfaces.
- Service Standards to include the requirements and targets for the service.
- Basic Terms and Conditions (such as the length of the contract, parties to the contract, scope of the contract and any basic definitions).
- Workload or volume ranges within which the contract applies. There may be a need to renegotiate the contract if workload or volumes move outside the agreed range.
- Responsibilities and Dependencies incorporating a description of the agreed obligations of both the purchasing organisation and the supplier. Escalation triggers and responsibilities are an important element here.
- Management Information. The reporting requirements need to be clearly set out in terms of what is reported, how it is reported, who does the reporting and when it is reported. Contract performance is assessed on the basis of performance against certain Key Performance Indicators and it is important these are clearly understood and set out.

Other areas that ought to be included are:

- Business Continuity arrangements
- Security requirements
- Dispute Resolution procedure
- Pricing and payment terms (which may include incentives and penalties)
- Technical standards that must be adhered to
- Disclosure agreements
- Adherence to the purchasing organisation's Change Management process
- Agreement on how changes to the contract are flagged and negotiated
- Confidentiality clauses and agreement on ownership of intellectual property
- Termination rights for both the purchaser and the supplier
- Ongoing obligations following the end of the contract (such as legacy support)

The identification of business needs and the development and building of a business case

The Service Design stage of the Service Lifecycle is responsible for the identification of business needs and the development and building of a business case. The relevant business area(s) must be closely involved in this stage and throughout the lifecycle of the contract in order to ensure that the business needs are and continue to be met.

The business case should be developed in line with the organisation's corporate policy using the standard templates and development stages. Organisations should have clearly defined and documented procedures for business case submission and approval. Both the IT Service Provider and the relevant business area(s) should agree the contents of the business case and ensure that the business needs are documented correctly and translated correctly into IT requirements. Sign-off must be at the right level with the necessary budgetary approval obviously being vital.

An initial business case will incorporate options. These costed options will include producing the service internally, going to the external market for the whole service or a combination of both internal and external provision for the service. As well as costings, there needs to be an analysis of timescales, targets, benefits and risks for each option. In addition to adhering to the organisation's business case policy, it is also important to ensure that the Supplier Management supplier policy and strategy is reflected in the business case. Alongside the business case, a Statement of Requirement, as well as an Invitation to Tender, will need to be developed, documented and agreed.

The evaluation, selection and procurement of new suppliers and contracts including the negotiation and agreement of contracts

The Service Design stage of the Service Lifecycle is responsible for the evaluation, selection and procurement of new suppliers and contracts including the negotiation and agreement of contracts. The relevant business area(s) must be closely involved in this stage and throughout the lifecycle of the contract in order to ensure that the business needs are and continue to be met.

A number of areas of the organisation have to work closely together throughout this part of the process. These include the relevant business area(s), the IT Service Provider and the Finance Department as well as the Purchasing and Procurement teams. These areas will be collectively involved in the evaluation, selection and procurement of new suppliers as well as in the negotiation and agreement of contracts. Supplier Management must ensure that all these inputs are coordinated and managed.

The evaluation and procurement of new suppliers and contracts includes the initial identification of the method of purchase or procurement followed by the establishment of evaluation criteria. The evaluation criteria will include quality and cost as well as the degree to which a service is 'off the shelf'. It will also take into account the capabilities of potential suppliers as organisations and the capabilities of the staff they will make available.

When evaluating potential suppliers the organisation will want to know as much as possible about the suppliers, including evidence of their track record, their capabilities, their resources, their credit rating and their other customers. Once the evaluation criteria are in place, the alternative options can be evaluated and a selection can be made. Then the negotiation starts in earnest. Negotiation is required around most aspects of the contract but in particular in the areas of targets, penalties, responsibilities, terms and conditions, renewal, termination, extensions, timescales and disputes. Once the negotiation is successfully concluded, the contract with the supplier is agreed and awarded.

Some contracts are more flexible than others. Flexible contracts allow changes to be made during the course of the agreement with minimal renegotiation. Comprehensive contracts, on the other hand, are far more tightly controlled and rely on detailed terms and conditions to prevent disputes and have eventualities predicted and catered for. The degree of flexibility in a contract will be driven by the contribution that the service makes to the organisation and by the nature of the relationship between the organisation and the supplier.

Evaluation procedures should be documented and the process steps recorded for audit purposes. Unfortunately, there will be times when relations with a supplier break down and it is useful to go back to the original procurement process and decision to see if any lessons can be learnt for future procurements.

The evaluation process should be centred on the importance of the service to the organisation together with the costs and risks involved in operating the service. A risk assessment conducted prior to the contract agreement is important to both the IT Service Provider and the potential third-party supplier. Such a risk assessment will reveal and highlight the risks for both parties allowing these risks to be avoided or mitigated. Intangible as well as tangible risks should be included in the risk assessment. Intangible risks include reputational damage, while more tangible risks revolve around cost and operational issues, as well as the impact of changes in regulation or legislation.

The evaluation, selection and procurement of new contracts and suppliers starts with the business case documents together with the Statement of Requirement and the Invitation to Tender. Once the formal evaluation and selection of suppliers is concluded, the contract is agreed that includes all the terms and conditions. The introduction of the new supplier or contract can then commence. The speed with which all this can be achieved is dependent on the size and complexity of the contract in question, the type of relationship the organisation has or intends having with the supplier and the availability of resources to conduct the process. Resources need to be made available from the IT Service Provider, from the relevant business area(s), from the Finance Department, from the Purchasing and Procurement team, and from the organisation's legal department, as well as from the potential suppliers.

A decision may be taken to select a particular supplier because the organisation already has a relationship with that supplier. Sometimes supplier selection is influenced by strategic political thinking from within the business or the IT Service Provider. Whatever the driver is for selecting a particular supplier, the process should be recorded and transparent.

Organisations can use single suppliers for a particular service or use more than one supplier. Multisourcing tends to take place where the service being purchased does not involve too much development work. Where significant development work is required, the duplication of costs in using more than one supplier would be difficult to justify. An organisation may use multisourcing for a number of reasons, including the provision of continuity, encouraging competition between suppliers and the avoidance of becoming too dependent on a particular supplier. Where there are significant development or transition costs, then there is a strong driver for using one supplier or single sourcing.

Increasingly, organisations are entering into partnering relationships with suppliers. In order for this to occur, the organisation and the supplier will need to be prepared to reveal and discuss their long-term strategy and business objectives. The organisation and its supplier work closely together and there are far less of the hierarchical and sometime adversarial relations and tensions that have traditionally been seen in supplier relations.

Partnering relationships vary in the degree to which the organisation and the supplier become entwined and linked. In some closer partnership relationships staff may be exchanged temporarily or permanently between the organisation and the supplier. In order for a partnering relationship to work, both parties (the organisation and the supplier) should obtain value from the relationship.

Shared risk and reward characterises partnership relationships. The costs borne and risks undertaken by each party and the split or division of the award to be derived should be agreed from the outset. Investments costs will be split and agreement reached on how risks of changing market conditions are dealt with. There will be collective responsibility for service performance and the performance of the partnership now and into the future.

Partnership relationships see the two organisations becoming closer and more integrated particularly with regard to their processes. The supplier will gain a greater understanding of how the organisation works. This will be at a number of levels, including the culture and operating method of the organisation through to how its infrastructure fits together. The supplier is able to react more quickly to changing circumstances as this understanding increases because they are able to predict and understand their partner's attitude, reaction and approach.

The supplier obtains benefit and value through being in a stable relationship particularly with regard to financial stability and being able to invest more securely in its own and the partnership's future. The financial stability of the supplier also provides reassurance for the purchasing party in that they know that the supplier is going to be around for the long term. From an organisation's point of view, they do not want the worry or concern that comes with dealing with a supplier who is in a precarious financial position and who may not be around in the future.

There needs to be openness and good strategic alignment for partnership relationships to work. The objectives of the two organisations become linked and it is important that they both have the same business vision of the future, which in turn is represented by their strategies. The two organisations need to be open and honest concerning service performance, cost and the management of risks with no hidden agendas.

Over time their infrastructures will often become aligned and the risks of this need to be understood. There are potential advantages, as well as risks, to be achieved through economies of scale, compatibility of processes and reduced costs. Quite often the weak point of a jointly provided IT solution is the technical link between the organisation's infrastructure and the supplier's infrastructure. These links tend to be unique and bring risks. The more the two infrastructures are joined, the lower the risk in this area.

Partnership relationships are also characterised by a good and open information and communication flow between the two parties. Trust is built up over time allowing strategic intentions to be shared.

The establishment of new suppliers and contracts
The establishment of new suppliers and contracts will involve putting in place the supplier service and contract, together with updating the Service and Contract Database and any other relevant systems that are in place. There will be a transition of the new supplier or contract into the live environment and this has to be agreed and managed. Engagement criteria are also agreed and documented at this stage so that both the purchaser and the supplier know who the appropriate individuals are within the other organisation to talk to depending on the topic and the circumstances. Relationships start to develop from this stage and these relationships need to be managed.

Taking on of a new supplier or contract is an important decision for an organisation and needs to be handled correctly. The relevant and necessary updating of the Service and Contract Database should be undertaken via the Change Management process. This ensures that the impact of taking on a new supplier or contract is comprehensively assessed.

A risk assessment will have been undertaken earlier in the process. This needs to be reassessed as the contract and the supplier relationship develops. Risks need to be understood, documented and managed. The level of risk will vary from contract to contract, from supplier to supplier and from service to service. Risk assessments and the associated Business Impact Analysis should be conducted in close liaison with IT Service Continuity Management, Information Security Management and Availability Management. Risks to be assessed will include operational, regulatory and reputational.

When the risks have been identified and managed, and the Supplier and Contract Database has been updated, the new supplier or contract can be put in place. The contact hierarchy will be established and publicised within both the purchasing organisation and the supplier organisation.

The categorisation of suppliers and contracts including risk assessment
It is clear that some suppliers are more important than others to an organisation. Suppliers need to be categorised in order to channel and target resources to where the Supplier Management is of most benefit. This is usually done in terms of risk and impact. The activities undertaken during supplier and contract categorisation include their assessment, both initial and ongoing. The Supplier and

Contract Database is updated and maintained and all service changes are moved forward and managed by Service Transition.

(The categorisation of suppliers and contracts is covered in more detail in the next section: The use of Supplier Categorisation and maintenance of the Supplier and Contract Database.)

The management of supplier and contract performance

The management of supplier and contract performance includes the management of the delivery of service from suppliers and the management of supplier's contribution to services. The quality of service and cost of service is monitored, and reports are produced in accordance with the service requirements. Once these reports are received, they are analysed in terms of service quality and service cost in order to see if improvements can be identified or shortcomings eliminated.

All aspects of the supplier relationship need to be managed throughout the lifecycle of the contract or relationship. Communication, escalation, contact information, changes and improvements all need to be managed. There should be a regular formal review of the relationship or contract as well as ongoing day-to-day management of the supplier or contract. This may take place annually or more frequently for some relationships. As the contract or relationship reaches the end of its term or lifespan, plans should be put in place for possible renewal, renegotiation, extension or termination. If a replacement contract or supplier is being considered, this activity should be a trigger for the evaluation, selection and procurement of new suppliers and contracts, including the negotiation and agreement of contracts stage of the supplier or contract lifecycle.

The degree of day-to-day management required will depend on a number of factors, including the importance of the service and the level of integration between the purchasing organisation and the supplier. If, for example, the supplier has to adhere to the purchasing organisation's Change Management process, an assessment of conformance should be undertaken using the necessary metrics and reporting tools. Likewise the link between the organisation's Service Desk and the third-line support provided by the supplier will need to be assessed. If the supplier is responsible for updating the purchasing organisation's Configuration Management System in respect of the Configuration Items it is responsible for, then, again, an assessment of compliance to the process will be needed by Supplier Management.

It is important that there are established and understood communication channels in place between the purchasing organisation and the supplier. As the relationship matures, understanding between the purchasing organisation and the supplier will increase, which may in turn lead to a closer relationship.

There are two types of structured review that should take place during the lifecycle of a contract:

- **Service, Service Scope and Contract Reviews:** These are reviews to ensure that the contract or supplier relationship is still pertinent to the present business needs of the organisation. Such reviews are conducted on a regular basis (usually annually) and are used to ensure that value for money is still being derived from the contract.

- **Service and Supplier Performance Reviews:** These reviews focus on the performance of the supplier over a particular period. The frequency of these reviews will be dictated by the importance of the supplier to the organisation, the level of risk and the criticality of the service that the supplier provides or supports. The more important the supplier, the more granular the reporting required.

As well as the structured formal reviews of performance, there may well be, depending on the size and importance of the contract, other regular performance reviews that will look at detailed service performance against the service targets, any complaints over the period, any escalations over the period, and Major Incident and Problem reviews, as well as any feedback from business areas or customers. For a large contract, these items may be reviewed in detail separately and then amalgamated for a formal review.

Another area that should be discussed and reviewed regularly with suppliers is forthcoming changes. These may be changes that directly impact the contract and the service that the supplier provides or supports, or wider significant changes within the organisation that the supplier ought to be aware of in order to ensure that any dependencies are understood and managed. Likewise, there may be changes taking place in the supplier organisation that would be useful for the purchasing organisation to know about. Forthcoming important business events or periods of high business activity will be highlighted and discussed.

Service Improvement Programmes (SIPs) will be formally discussed. Once an agreement on a SIP is reached, it may well be managed away from the regular performance meetings, but updates on progress will be required on a regular basis. SIPs may be initiated reactively to tackle areas of concern or weakness, or proactively in order to prevent future issues and improve the level of service.

There should be clear ownership of each supplier relationship within the purchasing organisation. Managing the relationship with a supplier should be the responsibility of one specific individual within the purchasing organisation. Depending on the size and scope of the contract, there may be many levels and points of regular interaction between the purchaser and the supplier, but the overall responsibility for the relationship from the purchaser's point of view must be vested with one identifiable individual. This is the Supplier Manager and they may be responsible for more than one supplier.

The Supplier Manager will ensure that all contact and interfaces with the supplier are understood and that they adhere to the overall governance framework for the relationship. Contact and decision-making criteria will be defined at various levels. The amount of time and effort put into managing a particular supplier or contract should be proportional to the importance of the supplier or contract to the organisation. Suppliers of less important services should not be micro-managed, allowing time to be allocated to managing the relationships with more important strategic suppliers. This means that time and effort is allocated in accordance with the potential value at stake.

It is important that the purchasing organisation does not lose sight of the need to maximise value from the contract or supplier relationship. It is the responsibility of Supplier Management to ensure that the business needs and the priorities of the organisation are matched and supported by the supplier's priorities. Value to the organisation can be derived from a contract or supplier relationship in a number of ways. These include improved performance, lower cost, robust Change Management, efficient handing of exceptions and transfer of skills and knowledge from the supplier to the purchasing organisation.

The original business case for adopting a particular supplier or contract should be revisited on a regular basis. There is a risk that while handling the day-to-day issues of Supplier Management, the bigger picture is missed as time goes on. The organisation requires Supplier Management to ensure that the benefits envisaged at the outset of the contract or relationship are measured and realised. This cannot be done in a vacuum: the wider changes in the business, technical and operating environments should be taken into consideration. If a particular envisaged benefit has not been realised, it may be that the operating environment has changed. Where this is the case the benefits, expectations and business case need to be revisited for the future taking into account the changed environment.

Satisfaction surveys are a tool that organisations can use in order to gauge the customers' or users' perception of a service. They are useful for obtaining the views of the people actually using the service. The views of customers who pay for the service and of users who use the service are both valid. However, it should be remembered that often, if users are asked what they expect, they would like to see the fastest, most up-to-date service etc., while customers are more concerned about value for money. Therefore, an understanding of the intended audience is crucial when designing, targeting and analysing the results of satisfaction surveys.

Historically, supplier relationships have at times been confrontational. This happens less often now as both parties understand the benefits of working together. The contract provides the framework for this cooperation. The building of long-term relationships requires time and effort and for this reason organisations may limit themselves to a small number of strategic suppliers. By entering into longer term relationships, both parties are aiming at shared risk and reward rather than short-term benefits for one particular party. This approach usually has more potential for generating value from the relationship than an approach that is more confrontational in nature.

The management and resolution of disputes
Even with less confrontational approaches to supplier relations, there will still be disputes that need to be sorted out. Hopefully, 'allocation of blame' sessions can be avoided and resolutions found that are acceptable to both parties. The terms of the contract should clearly set out the process to be followed when handling disputes. It is important that the right people from both the purchasing organisation and the supplier are involved. They should be individuals with sufficient seniority to make

decisions and should have a good understanding of the long-term benefits of the contract and the relationship.

The renewal or termination of contracts

At the end of contracts or at the agreed end of a supplier relationship, future requirements should be ascertained, documented and reviewed. The benefits accrued during the lifetime of the contract or supplier relationship should be ascertained and analysed. A decision is taken to either renew or to terminate the contract or relationship. Where the contract or relationship is to be renewed, this should be a trigger for the evaluation, selection and procurement of new suppliers and contracts. This will include the negotiation and agreement of the contracts stage of the supplier or contract lifecycle.

There are a number of things to consider when reviewing contracts. The performance of the contract to date and its future relevance are important. There may be alterations required to the contract. These alterations may be due to how the supplier has performed, how the purchasing organisation has changed or how the wider environment in which the service being delivered has changed. Changes may be made to targets within the contract, key contact points, or any part of the terms and conditions that are no longer valid. For complex contracts, the negotiation period may be protracted, but it is important that everything is agreed and documented in order to keep the contract and the relationship on a proper basis.

Renewal or termination discussions may be influenced by how both the purchasing organisation and the supplier view the future for the relationship. It may be that a relationship is getting closer, with the two parties becoming more integrated, or, on the other hand, one of the parties may view the relationship as winding down. The purchasing organisation may have changed the way that they source or procure services leading to a different future contract. The purchasing organisation will also want to compare the supplier's performance with other potential suppliers in order to ensure that value is still being maximised.

There are a number of actions and activities that should be undertaken where an organisation is looking to change supplier. There needs to be a robust risk assessment for the proposed change of supplier. This assessment will look at the risks of staying with the existing supplier, the risks of using a different supplier and the risks of migrating from one supplier to another. Exit costs have to be calculated properly in order for a financial comparison to be accurately made between what is on offer from a potential new supplier and what the present supplier has delivered and can deliver in the future. There will also be migration and take on costs for any new supplier. There may be costs other than financial when moving from one supplier to another, such as a period of degraded services. Often there is a period where both suppliers are used as the migration takes place, with the accompanying cost implications. All these things need to be taken into account.

The purchasing organisation would have involved their legal and procurement teams when drawing up and agreeing the contract, and they should also be involved with the renewal of a contract, particularly if there are changes, or the termination of the contract.

THE USE OF SUPPLIER CATEGORISATION AND MAINTENANCE OF THE SUPPLIER AND CONTRACT DATABASE

Main book reference: SD 4.7.5.2

The Supplier and Contract Database is the repository for all the important information held on suppliers and contracts.

SUPPLIER AND CONTRACT DATABASE

A database or structured document used to manage supplier contracts through-out their lifecycle. The Supplier and Contract Database contains the key attributes of all contracts with Suppliers, and should be part of the Service Knowledge Management System.

It is crucial that the Supplier and Contract Database is up to date and can be easily accessed by those who need to use it and who are authorised to use it. Access control is important because the Supplier and Contract Database will hold details of commercial information that will not be widely available within the organisation.

The use of a comprehensive and up-to-date Supplier and Contract Database gives Supplier Management a holistic view across all supplier activity. If there are pre-ferred suppliers or suppliers where a strategic partnership is planned, this will be indicated allowing the organisation to further its strategy and identify where the most value can be gained.

Suppliers are categorised according to their importance allowing Supplier Management to identify the important and strategic contracts and relationships. This means that not too much time and effort is spent on managing contracts and supplier relationships that do not add much value to the organisation. Categorisation is based on the importance of a supplier and the services it supplies to the business. This is illustrated in Figure 11.3.

The diagram shows that as risk and impact increase, the importance of the supplier to the organisation increases. Four different categories of supplier appear on the diagram:

- **Commodity Suppliers:** These are suppliers who provide low-value products that could easily be sourced elsewhere (such as racking or printer cartridges).

- **Operational Suppliers:** These are suppliers of operational services (such as print services).

- **Tactical Suppliers:** These are suppliers who are important to the business and who provide services that the business relies on. Maintenance contracts are often with tactical suppliers.

- **Strategic Suppliers:** These are suppliers with whom a potential partnering arrangement has been identified and then put in place. These tend to be long term with integration between the purchasing organisation and the supplier. Network provision is an often used example.

Figure 11.3 Supplier categorisation (Source: OGC ITIL Service Design ISBN 978-0-113310-47-0)

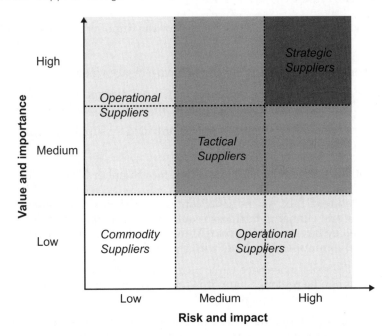

The Commodity Suppliers should have the least amount of time and effort directed towards the management of their contracts and relationship, while the Strategic Suppliers will be the main focus for Supplier Management. Strategic Suppliers are those who are most valuable to the business and where the risk and impact is greatest. The more strategic a supplier becomes, the more the business areas will want to be and need to be involved in the management of the contract and the relationship. While the Supplier Manager will own the relationship, there will be significant business input into the development of the relationship.

Risk increases if the purchasing company procures services from a supplier that are bespoke or have been customised at the purchaser's request. Standard services are more like commodities, while bespoke or customised services are far more difficult to replace. Suppliers become more difficult to remove as they become more strategic. Bespoke or tailored services increase the dependency on the supplier.

Supplier Management activity can be time-consuming especially when dealing with a large number of different suppliers, so there are drivers for organisations to reduce the number of suppliers that they use. In some cases, organisations reduce the number of suppliers to one prime supplier. This makes the supplier management more straightforward, but there are obvious risks of being so dependent on one particular supplier, and these risks have to be understood and managed.

KEY METRICS, CHALLENGES, CRITICAL SUCCESS FACTORS AND RISKS

Main book references: SD 4.7.7, 4.7.9

The most important Critical Success Factors for the Supplier Management process are:

- all supplier relationships and contracts have a clear owner;
- the business activities of the organisation are not disrupted or degraded by lack of availability or other issues brought about by supplier performance;
- the services provided or input to services provided by suppliers is in line with the needs of the business areas.

The following lists some of the challenges that face Supplier Management:

- A constant state of flux. As one set of contracts are being negotiated and agreed, new and changing business requirements are appearing. This can be mitigated by having good Service Management processes in place and by having good communication links with the business areas.

- Delivering the existing service while negotiating future contracts. Contract negotiations can be prolonged and it is important not to lose sight of the need to continue to deliver the current services.

- Dealing with and managing contracts that are not as good as they should be. Contracts are often inherited and some may lack the rigour that Supplier Management would like to see. Where this is the case, it is important to have a good working relationship with the supplier because it may be that the contract cannot be relied on if there are service issues.

- Disagreements over charges or penalties. This is why it is important that the contract is properly negotiated and drawn up in the first place, with the charging criteria clearly set out.

- Personality conflicts. The contract has clearly set out roles and responsibilities, so it should provide a framework for interfacing between the two parties. If there are personality conflicts, it is important that the Supplier Manager (with the ultimate responsibility for the relationship) is able to ensure that the service continues to be delivered in accordance with the needs of the business.

A number of Key Performance Indicators and metrics can be used by Supplier Management in order to assess the performance of the process. As always, the process should be measured in terms that are meaningful from a business point of view. Supplier Management is in place to ensure that business value is maximised. The metrics and Key Performance Indicators should reflect this.

Important Supplier Management metrics include:

- reduction in the number of breaches in contracts;
- increase in the number of suppliers meeting contract targets;
- increase in the number of contracts with nominated contract managers;
- increase in the number of suppliers with nominated supplier managers;
- increase in the number of contract reviews conducted.

These metrics help to assess the effectiveness and efficiency of the Supplier Management process and help to underpin the Key Performance Indicators, which are:

- third-party services and targets aligned with the needs of the business;
- business protected from poor performance from suppliers;
- service availability not disrupted by supplier performance;
- clear ownership of contracts.

The risks that face Supplier Management include:

- a state of flux in either the IT Service Provider or the supplier (or both) leading to a lack of communication and relationship building;
- a lack of resources in the organisation to conduct robust Supplier Management;
- a lack of commitment to the Supplier Management process from senior management and budget holders;
- bypassing of the process, with elements of the IT Service Provider discussing and negotiating directly with suppliers without the knowledge of Supplier Management;
- contracts that tie the IT Service Provider into an agreement that is no longer appropriate for the organisation;
- unhelpful suppliers and supplier representatives.

INPUTS AND OUTPUTS

Main book reference: SD 4.7.6

The inputs to the Supplier Management process include the following:

- Service Portfolio Management providing information on proposed new services that will require Supplier Management activity.
- Service Catalogue Management, along with Configuration Management, will have updates that will be useful to Supplier Management.

- IT Security Management provides the IT Service Provider's security policy and specific security requirements relating to suppliers.

- Configuration Management will provide input to the Supplier Management process concerning the updating of the Configuration Management System and where responsibilities lie in this regard.

- Service Level Management will have responsibility for the maintenance and management of the Service Level Agreements that are underpinned by the contracts with third parties. There will be a steady information flow between Service Level Management and Supplier Management and a regular dialogue between the two areas.

- Financial Management will provide information on the cost of supplier services together with future budgets and plans.

- Incident and Problem Management will provide details of Incidents and Problems that relate to supplier performance.

- Availability Management will input details of availability issues caused by supplier performance.

- Service Continuity Management will input requirements for all third-party delivered services, particularly where the continuity site is an externally owned site.

- Service Strategy provides supplier plans and strategy.

- Business information from the organisation's business plans and likely future direction.

The outputs from the Supplier Management process include the following:

- The Supplier and Contract Database
- Supplier Service Improvement Plans
- Minutes of Supplier and Contract Review meetings
- Supplier Survey reports
- Triggers for Continual Service Improvement in other areas
- Knowledge gained from suppliers that can be spread wider within the organisation.

12 FINANCIAL MANAGEMENT

INTRODUCTION

Financial Management is concerned with ensuring that the organisation's financial resources are properly looked after. Organisations need to manage their financial resources effectively in order to compete and to survive. This is especially the case for commercial organisations, but it is also the case for non-commercial organisations who will need to justify their value and their worth.

FINANCIAL MANAGEMENT

Financial Management consists of the Function and Processes responsible for managing an IT Service Provider's Budgeting, Accounting and charging requirements.

The business areas, as well as IT, require quantification in money terms of the value of IT services and the assets used to deliver these services. Financial Management provides this, together with an understanding of the costs of potential future services and investments. Much of the work of Financial Management is centred on understanding the value of services allowing comparisons to be made and highlighting the cost and value implications of any changes to services.

In order to be able to quickly react to changing circumstances, organisations must be able to be in a position to make rapid decisions based on an accurate understanding of present costs and potential future costs. Under robust Financial Management, costs are highlighted and controlled, the value of services is identified and realised, and investment decisions are made on the basis of a proper cost and value assessment.

Organisations need to have the right amount of money available in order to action their plans. They must track and understand how money has been spent, as well as ascertaining whether the money has been spent effectively. Potential new investments have to be understood in terms of their cost and the value they will provide over time. The cost of delivering services has to be clearly understood in order to allow that cost to be allocated to those who use the service if appropriate. Where demand changes, the calculation of the allocation of costs will need to be revised quickly in order to retain a fair apportionment.

Financial Management ensures that organisations have an understanding of the cost of what they are doing, how these costs are made up and what influences them. It is able to put a value on the services delivered to business areas and, if appropriate, provide a pricing mechanism and method for charging.

There are close links between Financial Management and Service Portfolio Management. They work together in order to ensure that potential future investments and investment options are fully understood in terms of cost and value to the organisation. Increasingly costs of IT Service provision are becoming more transparent, particularly where charges are detailed in the Service Catalogue.

Financial Management is used by organisations:

- to improve their decision making;
- to understand the value of services;
- to exert financial compliance and control;
- to understand the cost and value of potential future investments;
- to allow the cost of changes to be highlighted and managed;
- to exert operational control.

The tracking of expenditure is a key role for Financial Management. Budgets are produced and expenditure is then tracked against these budgets. Variances between budget and actual expenditure are highlighted, queried and managed.

PURPOSE, GOAL AND OBJECTIVES

Main book references: SS 5.1 up to 5.1.2

The purpose of Financial Management is to ensure that:

- the financial assets or resources of the organisation are managed;
- the financial assets or resources are allocated in such a way as to support and align with the organisation's plans and the requirements of the business areas;
- financial risks are identified and managed effectively;
- investment decisions are made on the basis of a good understanding of costs and potential value, and how that potential value links to the business objectives of the organisation;
- clear accountability and governance arrangements are in place;
- financial regulatory policies and corporate financial guidelines are adhered to.

The goal of Financial Management is to ensure that the best use is made of the organisation's financial resources and that the relevant regulatory requirements and corporate governance rules are adhered to.

The key objectives of Financial Management are:

- to ensure that there is a process in place for financial planning and budgeting that is both efficient and effective;
- to make sure that the costs and value of all IT services, processes and activities are monitored and measured;
- to ensure that all proposed investments have a business case;
- to make sure that all financial risks are clearly identified and then managed;
- to ensure that there is an audit process in place and to make sure that all financial expenditure is properly accounted for;
- to make sure that there is a financial governance framework in place and to ensure that the accountabilities of budget holders are understood;
- to ensure that all financial plans and the division of budgets are in line with the Service Portfolio.

OBJECTIVE

The defined purpose or aim of a Process, an Activity or an organisation as a whole. Objectives are usually expressed as measurable targets. The term Objective is also informally used to mean a requirement.

THE SCOPE OF THE PROCESS

Main book references: SS 5.1.2 up to 5.1.2.1

The scope of Financial Management is wide. It is involved with all services, all processes and all activities. It has a key contribution to make throughout the Service Lifecycle by providing the information that will drive decision making. The information produced by Financial Management is used across the whole organisation and underpins all decision-making processes. Financial Management pulls together many data inputs from areas within the organisation, it translates these inputs into meaningful outputs and then aids other areas in understanding the outputs and how they can be used to make decisions and to track the value generated by previous decisions.

THE CONCEPT OF SERVICE VALUATION

Main book references: SS 5.1.2.1, 5.1.3.1, Figure 5.3

Financial Management provides a common language that is understood by the business. Service Valuation goes further and allows the business areas to see what is actually being delivered to them in terms of what it is worth to them. Service Valuation quantifies in financial terms the funding required in order for services to be delivered. Services can be made up of many components and Financial Management needs to assign a value to each of these components in order to be able to quickly ascertain the value of any combination of components. This is useful information for business areas that will be looking at potential investments in services.

The business areas view the world in terms of the services they receive. Traditionally, IT areas have focused more on individual components. That has changed and is changing, so that both the IT Service Provider and the business areas can talk the same language in terms of services and their value. That said, in order to be able to do this, the IT Service Provider has to have an in-depth understanding of the cost and value of each of its components.

Financial Management centres on quantifying the value of services and of the assets that underpin their delivery. This is Service Valuation. There are two components that make up Service Valuation: the Service Provisioning Value and the Service Value Potential (see Figure 12.1).

Figure 12.1 Customer assets are the basis for defining value (Source: OGC ITIL Service Strategy ISBN 978-0-113310-45-6)

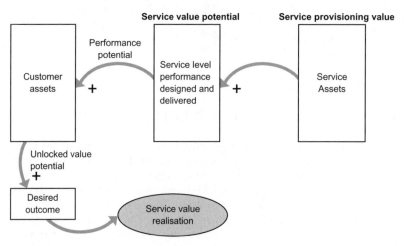

The Service Provisioning Value is the actual underlying cost to the IT Service Provider relating to the provision of a service. This includes the cost of all the components that make up the service. The Service Provisioning Value is the sum of the actual costs of delivering the service. Cost elements will include:

- hardware;
- software;
- software licences;

- maintenance fees;
- charges for data centre;
- facilities costs;
- personnel costs;
- compliance costs.

This is a similar approach to the traditional cost model. The sum of the costs provides a baseline that allows the calculation of the minimum value of the service. IT Service Providers will not usually want to provide a service where the full provisioning cost cannot be recovered.

The Service Value Potential is the added value of the service based on what the customer perceives to be the financial benefit. Figure 12.1 shows how the total value of a service is derived by adding together the Service Provisioning Value and the Service Value Potential. This value, when combined with the assets of the customer, allows the value potential to be unlocked and service value realised. While the Service Provisioning Value is more transparent and is easier to calculate than the Service Value Potential, there are a number of techniques now available to help with the identification of Service Value Potential.

Aggregating the Service Provisioning Value and the Service Value Potential, to give the total value of the service, means that the IT Service Provider can provide service information that is immediately recognisable and understandable to potential and existing customers and business areas. The common language based on services enables both the IT Service Provider and the business areas to understand what is being delivered and what it is worth. Additionally, where the service is being charged for, both the IT Service Provider and the business areas can see what a fair price would be.

When considering Service Valuation, there are a number of decisions that need to be made on the method of calculation. The first of these is the debate about whether costs are direct or indirect. For some costs, the answer will be fairly obvious, but for others the decision might not be so straightforward.

COST

The amount of money spent on a specific Activity, IT Service or business unit. Costs consist of real cost (money), notional cost (such as people's time) and depreciation.

DIRECT COST

The cost of providing an IT Service that can be allocated in full to a specific Customer, Cost Centre, Project etc. For example, the cost of providing non-shared servers or software licences.

INDIRECT COST

That part of the Cost of producing an IT Service that cannot be allocated in full to a specific customer. For example, the cost of providing shared servers or software licences. An Indirect Cost is also known as an overhead.

Each of the cost components should be first identified and then the organisation will require rules and guidelines in order to be able to fairly and openly decide whether a cost can be attributed to a specific area or split between areas. Where it is to be split between areas, the percentage allocated to each area will have to be decided. The governing principle should be what is perceived to be seen as fair.

Decisions also need to be made on the allocation of labour costs. If the Human Resources department has one individual dedicated to a particular business unit, then their labour costs will be a fixed cost that can be attributed to that business area. However, most staff in centralised departments conduct work for more than one business area. Tracking exactly how their time is spent is not always easy.

The translation from cost account data to service value can only be achieved when costs are linked to services rather then being linked to cost accounts. Figure 12.2 shows an example of cost account data being translated into service costs and then service value.

This translation allows the cost and value of services to be far more apparent to the IT Service Provider and to the purchasing business areas. It is important to be able to put a monetary value on utility optimisations and warranty enhancements in order to arrive at a service potential added value. Putting a price on this service potential added value can be tricky, but the IT Service Provider and the customers are now getting far more of an insight into the value of services as well as the cost.

Variable cost elements are not set or fixed but fluctuate based on the number of transactions or the number of users as opposed to fixed cost elements that do not vary with IT Service usage.

VARIABLE COST

A cost that depends on how much the IT Service is used, how many products are produced, the number and type of users, or something else that cannot be fixed in advance.

FIXED COST

A cost that does not vary with IT Service usage. An example would be the cost of server hardware.

Figure 12.2 The translation between cost account data, service costs and service value (Source: OGC ITIL Service Strategy ISBN 978-0-113310-45-6)

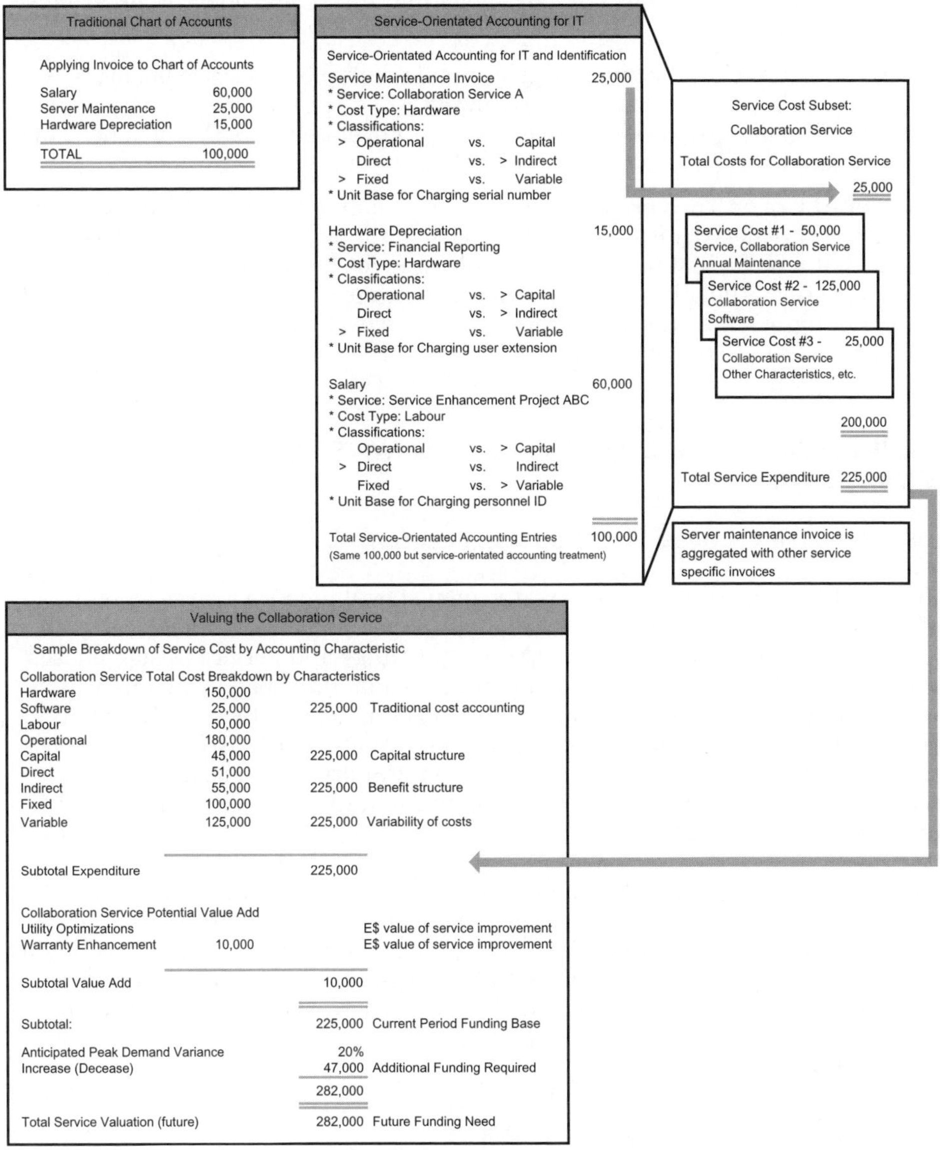

Traditional Chart of Accounts

Applying Invoice to Chart of Accounts

Salary	60,000
Server Maintenance	25,000
Hardware Depreciation	15,000
TOTAL	100,000

Service-Orientated Accounting for IT

Service-Orientated Accounting for IT and Identification

Service Maintenance Invoice   25,000
* Service: Collaboration Service A
* Cost Type: Hardware
* Classifications:
    > Operational   vs.   Capital
      Direct   vs.   > Indirect
    > Fixed   vs.   Variable
* Unit Base for Charging serial number

Hardware Depreciation   15,000
* Service: Financial Reporting
* Cost Type: Hardware
* Classifications:
      Operational   vs.   > Capital
      Direct   vs.   > Indirect
    > Fixed   vs.   Variable
* Unit Base for Charging user extension

Salary   60,000
* Service: Service Enhancement Project ABC
* Cost Type: Labour
* Classifications:
      Operational   vs.   > Capital
    > Direct   vs.   Indirect
      Fixed   vs.   > Variable
* Unit Base for Charging personnel ID

Total Service-Orientated Accounting Entries   100,000
(Same 100,000 but service-orientated accounting treatment)

Service Cost Subset:
Collaboration Service

Total Costs for Collaboration Service   25,000

Service Cost #1 - 50,000
Service, Collaboration Service
Annual Maintenance

Service Cost #2 - 125,000
Collaboration Service
Software

Service Cost #3 -   25,000
Collaboration Service
Other Characteristics, etc.

    200,000

Total Service Expenditure   225,000

Server maintenance invoice is aggregated with other service specific invoices

Valuing the Collaboration Service

Sample Breakdown of Service Cost by Accounting Characteristic

Collaboration Service Total Cost Breakdown by Characteristics

Hardware	150,000		
Software	25,000	225,000	Traditional cost accounting
Labour	50,000		
Operational	180,000		
Capital	45,000	225,000	Capital structure
Direct	51,000		
Indirect	55,000	225,000	Benefit structure
Fixed	100,000		
Variable	125,000	225,000	Variability of costs
Subtotal Expenditure		225,000	

Collaboration Service Potential Value Add

Utility Optimizations		E$ value of service improvement
Warranty Enhancement	10,000	E$ value of service improvement
Subtotal Value Add	10,000	
Subtotal:	225,000	Current Period Funding Base
Anticipated Peak Demand Variance	20%	
Increase (Decease)	47,000	Additional Funding Required
	282,000	
Total Service Valuation (future)	282,000	Future Funding Need

Variable cost elements need to be identified. Business areas need to budget ahead, and in order to do so, they prefer to have predictable costs. While the fluctuations in variable costs are within their control (i.e. it is due to their users or their transactions), they are not always easy to predict. In order to provide business areas with predictable costs, there are a number of methods that can be adopted by the IT Service Provider:

- **A Maximum Cost:** This involves costing the service at the maximum level of variability. This means that the business areas will not receive any 'nasty surprises', but in reality they are being overcharged and will later benefit from rebates. Depending on their budgeting rules, some business areas may prefer this.

- **An Average Cost:** Again, this gives predictability because the business area is able to budget with confidence. However, in due course, when the costing period finishes, there will be some under- or over-charging that will need to be addressed.

- **Tiered Costs:** The variations in usage are analysed in order to identify any natural breaks (tiers) so costs are applied at different rates for the different tiers. It may be that a service is heavily used for five days in a week and has lower use on the other two days. Tiered costs means that budgeting becomes easier for business areas and they are able to easily identify the potential cost savings from reducing usage.

THE IMPORTANCE OF THE PROCESS TO THE SERVICE LIFECYCLE AND BUSINESS VALUE

Main book references: SS 5.1 opening section, 5.1.1

Financial Management, when correctly applied, will produce a large amount of useful information that can be used at all stages of the Service Lifecycle. Decisions that are made during the Service Strategy and Service Design phases of the Service Lifecycle are dependent on the availability of accurate financial information. Likewise, through Service Transition and into Service Operation, Financial Management will provide data that can be used to assess the progress of the service. Continual Service Improvement initiatives will be driven by the cost information made available from Financial Management together with a desire for greater quality.

Organisations will want to know which are their most expensive services and why. They will also want to understand which are their most efficient services. Financial Management will be the source of this information. Lack of meaningful Financial Management would mean that organisations would be making decisions 'blind', hoping that the outcome they wish for will be achieved, but without any understanding of the underlying costs.

ASPECTS AND CONCEPTS OF THE PROCESS

Main book references: SS 5.1.2.5, 5.1.2.6, 5.1.2.7, 5.1.4.2

Funding
Financial Management is in place in order to ensure that there is proper funding for the delivery and consumption of services. It is important to plan ahead so that planned activity is matched with available funds.

PLANNING

An activity responsible for creating one or more plans. For example, Financial Management planning.

Financial Management Planning looks at variances in supply and demand that are the result of business strategy. It is, therefore, crucial to have the necessary information from internal areas, suppliers and customers in the business areas. Service Valuation information is used to predict or forecast the future cost of delivery against a pattern of changing demand as expressed by Demand Modelling. The Financial Management process looks at the necessary data to change service costs and patterns of demand into financial resourcing requirements.

It is important that Financial Management works closely with Service Portfolio Management in order to ensure that all services within the Service Catalogue are included in the Financial Planning process. Financial Planning information is used to enable the organisation to look in detail at the costs and potential efficiency saving for all services. Servicing Provisioning Optimisation looks at all the financial inputs and constraints around a service in order to ascertain whether it could be delivered more efficiently (either internally or using an external third-party supplier).

For many or most organisations, Financial Planning will relate to a fixed period or budget period. Financial Planning information combined with future income information will be translated into a budget.

BUDGET

A list of all the money an organisation or business unit plans to receive, and plans to pay out, over a specified period of time.

BUDGETING

The Activity of predicting and controlling the spending of money. Budgeting consists of a periodic negotiation cycle to set future Budgets (usually annual) and the day-to-day monitoring and adjusting of current Budgets.

The deliverable from Financial Planning is a Financial Plan or a budget. This budget will be for a clearly defined time period, usually one year. The budget will include expected income and expected expenditure, split into different categories over the time period. Financial Management will be able to track actual performance against budget by highlighting expenditure and by splitting it into different categories. This allows financial control to be exerted.

The budget must contain details of costs for all activities. This will include services being delivered, services being developed and services being retired, as well as new projects, investments and planned changes. The budget will also illustrate how costs and income are likely to vary throughout the relevant period. Seasonal variations can be incorporated in this way. A budget should not be an aspirational goal, rather it should be based on what is realistic. Budgets may not turn out to have been as accurate as desired, but they should reflect the best prediction possible at the time taking into account all the available information. Budgets will often be made without complete information and without knowing what changes may occur in the operating environment, so some contingency should be built in.

The amount or degree of contingency should be relative to the risk of budget variations. A service being offered in an atmosphere with volatile demand can justifiably have more contingency built into its budget than a service that operates in a more stable demand environment.

The total operating costs for the IT Service Provider will be the sum of the operating costs for all services in the Service Catalogue and the costs for new or changing services in the Service Pipeline. There may also be costs in relation to retention of functionality for retired services.

There are three main categories or areas that make up Financial Planning:

- **Demand:** The present and future demand for services needs to be understood together with the factors that influence that demand. Service Valuation information is used to predict the cost of service delivery against a pattern of changing demand.

- **Operating and Capital:** All future operating and capital expenditure should be taken into account. The approach is similar because both require close liaison with the business areas to ensure that all planned expenditure is understood and recorded. Capital expenditure will have an impact on the organisation's asset levels, which in turn will need to be understood by their accountant and auditors.

- **Regulatory and Environmental:** There will be a regulatory framework within the organisation that Financial Management will need to adhere to. This will include any statutory reporting with the timescales and format defined. Within this framework, Financial Management will put in place internal processes, including audits, in order to ensure the regulatory requirements are met.

OPERATIONAL COST

Cost resulting from running IT Services. These are often repeating payments. For example, staff costs, hardware maintenance and electricity (also known as current expenditure or revenue expenditure).

CAPITAL EXPENDITURE

The cost of purchasing something that will become a financial asset, for example computer equipment and buildings. The value of the asset is depreciated over multiple accounting periods.

The rules for the regulatory framework within an organisation will come from the business. One area that is often highlighted is the need to budget and plan for ongoing maintenance charges when purchasing fixed assets. The organisation's policy on depreciation will also be set out. Financial Management will be tasked with monitoring income and expenditure against plans and budgets with variances being highlighted and managed.

Confidence in financial information is paramount. If areas of the organisation lack confidence in the financial information being provided, then the worth of that financial information is devalued. There needs to be a high level of statistical accuracy when converting the outputs of service-based demand modelling into clear financial requirements. Controls should be put in place to protect the integrity and accuracy of the financial information. This is important because the information will be used to make key business decisions.

Service Investment Analysis

Financial Management is responsible for evaluating proposals for investments to determine whether they make financial sense. The aim of Service Investment Analysis is to arrive at an indication of value for the whole lifecycle of a service taking into account the value received and the costs incurred.

All Service Investment Analysis should be conducted in an agreed standard manner and produced in an agreed standard format. Financial Management will set the rules for deciding the level of analysis required for a particular investment based on the cost and scale of the proposed investment. Assumptions will need to be made during Service Investment Analysis and again Financial Management should follow a standardised route of documenting assumptions and evaluating the risks to the accuracy of the decision-making process if the assumptions later prove to be incorrect. Good Financial Management will ensure that all potential proposals for investment have a clear case made for them. This normally takes the form of a business case.

Accounting

Regular monitoring against budgets is required in order to provide sound financial management. The results of this monitoring will indicate where income or expenditure in a particular area is higher or lower than expected. This enables action to be taken in order to maintain financial control.

ACCOUNTING

The process responsible for identifying actual Costs of delivering IT Services, comparing these with budgeted Costs, and managing variance from the Budget.

Where variances occur, reductions in expenditure or increases in income may be stipulated in order to bring the costs and income back in line with the budget. It may be that variations in one part of the budget can be offset against another part of the budget. Where this happens the budget will need to be adjusted. However, budgets should not just be changed because performance has not matched expectations. Budget variances need to be fully understood with the lessons learnt being fed into the ongoing budget and future budgets. For the wider organisation, performance against budget may determine whether proposed projects are put back or brought forward.

Income and expenditure are accounted for in Financial Management. The information is broken down to enable income and expenditure to be divided between customers, services and activities. This allows the cost-effectiveness of services to be derived.

COST EFFECTIVENESS

A measure of the balance between the effectiveness and the Cost of a Service, Process or Activity. A cost-effective process is one that achieves its objectives at minimum cost.

Effective and up-to-date cost-effectiveness information enables decisions to be made on the future of services. Value for money is an informal measure of cost-effectiveness.

VALUE FOR MONEY

An informal measure of Cost Effectiveness. Value for Money is often based on a comparison with the cost of alternatives.

The provision of accurate accounting information allows initial cost–benefit analysis to be ratified and future cost–benefit analysis to be underpinned by proven historic information.

COST–BENEFIT ANALYSIS

An Activity that analyses and compares the costs and the benefits involved in one or more alternative courses of action.

Financial Management will focus on services and on tracking the costs and income for those services. Cost account data is translated into service account information. This highlights the services and their management. Accounting will focus on Cost Types, Cost Classifications and Service Recording.

Cost Types
Cost Types are categories of expenditure, such as hardware, software, facilities and personnel. These are the terms of the traditional cost model and can also be related to services. Cost Types are then broken down into Cost Elements and then Cost Units.

Cost Classifications

Cost Classifications are used to indicate what the cost has been incurred for. The classifications include:

- **Capital and Operational Costs:** The organisation's financial governance will indicate how Capital and Operational costs are to be treated.

- **Direct and Indirect Costs:** The decision on whether a cost is direct or indirect dictates whether it can be assigned directly or indirectly to a service, customer or business area. Indirect costs will have to be split or shared across services, customers or business areas.

- **Fixed and Variable Costs:** The degree to which costs are variable will often depend on contracts that have been entered into and how long these contracts last. From a Financial Planning point of view, it is easier to be confident with future forecasts if the majority of costs are fixed.

- **Cost Units:** The lowest level of category to which costs are allocated or assigned and an identified unit of consumption.

Service Recording

Service Recording is the allocation of cost entries to the correct services. For some complex and well-defined services, there may be lower level allocations with the service being broken down further.

Chargeback

Whether or not to chargeback for services is a strategic decision within an organisation. Charging increases the accountability for the costs of services. It also boosts the visibility and transparency of these service costs. However, charging in itself is an overhead that will increase the operating costs of the IT Service Provider. One outcome of introducing chargeback for IT Services is that customers and business areas will easily be able to compare the cost and quality of the service they receive with what is being offered by competitors. Business areas will be able to assess alternatives in terms of cost and quality of what they receive from their internal IT Service Provider.

In the absence of charging, users, customers and business areas may view IT Service provision as being free. Where this is the case, they are not likely to use resources sparingly. The introduction of charging focuses the mind and aids the changing of attitudes to consumption.

Charging introduces a way in which to influence customer behaviour, allowing the shaping of demand and utilisation to match expensive or sparse capacity.

Chargeback brings visibility to the delivery of IT Services. The provision of a Service Portfolio and a Service Catalogue raises the profile of services and this is reinforced if the services are charged for in a clear and understandable manner. Without a clear view on services and their contribution to value, it is not easy to ascertain whether a charge is fair, which can lead to difficulties between the IT Service Provider and its customers in the business areas. Pricing is the mechanism for deciding how much to charge for services.

PRICING

The Activity for establishing how much customers will be charged.

Where chargeback is used to influence behaviour and patterns of demand, it is important to remember that the charging must add value and relate to business processes that are understandable. A charge per transaction is understandable from a business point of view, while a charge per unit of CPU is not. The charging should be as simplistic as the complexity of the organisation allows.

There are a number of Chargeback models. As well as simplicity, business areas will want predictability over charges and will want to understand how their behaviour and the behaviour of their users can influence the charges. Regardless of which Chargeback model is used, the ultimate objective of providing value to the business areas should not be lost.

The Chargeback models include:

- **Fixed or User Cost:** A simple model in which the total cost is divided by the number of users or number of outlets. However, with this method, there is no attempt to influence demand or to identify patterns of demand.

- **Notional Charging:** Customers and business areas are informed what they would be charged if a particular charging system was in place. This has the advantage of providing the visibility of costs without the overhead of invoicing and invoice collection. Notional Charging is often used as a transitional tool as organisations move from not charging for IT Services to a system where IT Services are charged back.

- **Metered Usage:** This requires the organisation to have the capability to measure the use of services accurately and to be able to allocate the relevant charge for that usage to the correct customer or business area.

- **Tiered Subscription:** This employs tiers in which various levels of warranty and utility are made available at each price level. The obvious example is the Service Desk that offers silver, gold and platinum levels of service at different rates. It can be difficult to break down utility and warranty to levels where incremental changes in them can be identified and charged for. Care is required in order to avoid making the charging model too complex.

- **Direct Plus:** In this model, those charges that can be directly attributed and allocated to customers are charged together with an additional charge that represents their share of the indirect costs. The apportionment of the indirect costs should be seen to be fair.

RETURN ON INVESTMENT AND THE BUSINESS CASE

Main book references: SS 5.2 up to 5.2.2.1, 5.2.3 up to 5.2.3.1

Return on Investment (ROI) is an important idea and method for assessing the value of an investment in financial terms. In Service Management, ROI is used to work out the value added by the use of an asset or assets. In its simplest form, it is calculated by dividing the value added by the cost of the asset.

RETURN ON INVESTMENT

A measurement of the expected benefit of an investment. In the simplest sense it is the net profit of an investment divided by the net worth of the assets invested in that investment.

The use of ROI lets an organisation set a specific percentage target to be achieved by all investment decisions. Care needs to be exercised here over the length of time allocated for the investment to generate the additional value. Selecting the correct timescale, which is a business decision, will have a large impact on whether an investment decision is made.

Understanding the Total Cost of Ownership (TCO) of an asset that may potentially be purchased gives a good indicator when compared with income throughout its lifecycle of whether the asset will add value.

TOTAL COST OF OWNERSHIP

A methodology used to help make investment decisions. Total Cost of Ownership assesses the full Lifecycle cost of owning a Configuration Item, not just the initial cost or purchase price.

Three areas need to be considered when viewing Return on Investment:

- Business Case
- Pre-programme Return on Investment
- Post-programme Return on Investment

These are discussed in the following sections.

Business Case
A Business Case is a decision support and planning tool that projects the likely consequences of a business action.

> **BUSINESS CASE**
>
> A justification for a significant item of expenditure. It includes information about Costs, benefits, options, risks and possible problems.

While the main thrust of the business case will be a financial analysis, non-financial considerations may be involved.

Financial Management will work with the business areas to assess the potential business return relative to the size of the investment. This potential business return represents the business impact that will be in support of a wider business objective. The timescale for benefits, together with the risks, contingencies, confidence in the data and sensitivity to change will all be included in a Business Case.

It is important that the Business Case clearly sets out the method used for assessing the benefits and costs as well as the assumptions made and the level of confidence in the figures used.

Pre-programme Return on Investment
Capital budgeting centres on spending money now in order to obtain future value and is important to Pre-programme Return on Investment Analysis. There tends to be two types of capital budgeting decision. Firstly, analysis of whether the likely future returns justify the capital expenditure now and, secondly, where two or more options are being considered and costs and potential returns are being compared.

Post-programme Return on Investment
The actual ROI after the asset has been purchased or the project completed needs to be known. The organisation will want to know if the expected value was achieved and what lessons can be learnt for future investments.

ACTIVITIES, METHODS AND TECHNIQUES

Main book reference: SS 5.1.3

The main activities of Budgeting, Accounting and Charging have been covered in the earlier section. As well as Service Valuation, there are other models and methods available to Financial Management. Analysis of the most effective method in which to deliver services will involve organisations looking at alternative models for the provision of services. Options include:

- **Managed Services:** These are services that are fully funded by the business area that uses them.

- **Shared Services:** These are more than one service delivered to business areas using a shared infrastructure.

- **Utility-based Provisioning:** This is a more advanced type of provisioning similar to shared services but with more services using the infrastructure.

- **Onshore, Offshore or Near Shore:** Different organisations will benefit in different ways from having services provided onshore, offshore or near shore. What may work for one organisation, may not work for another.

Service Provisioning Cost Analysis is the activity of ranking the various types of provisioning options in order to understand which one (or which mixture) would be right for the organisation.

There are three Funding Model alternatives:

- **Rolling Plan Funding:** When one cycle of funding completes, another cycle commences.

- **Trigger-based Plans:** Pre-agreed triggers set off the funding process. An example would be a major change.

- **Zero-based Funding:** Represents only funding the actual costs of the service.

Business Impact Analysis is used to identify an organisation's most critical services. Understanding Business Impact Analysis can lead to better decision making with decisions based on the actual impact on the business areas. Business Impact Analysis provides an assessment of impact translated into a financial value combined with an assessment of operational risk.

DESIGN AND IMPLEMENTATION

Main book reference: SS 5.1.4.3

There are five tracks that can be used as a check to ensure that the implementation of Financial Management is proceeding as intended. These tracks are Plan, Analyse, Design, Implement and Measure.

- **Plan:** The plan for the implementation of Financial Management will be drawn up with appropriate milestones and timescales. The plan should take into account the culture and complexity of the organisation. All inputs and outputs from Financial Management need to be identified and catered for. Funding for the implementation will be required and decisions on the tools and systems will need to be taken.

- **Analyse:** This stage is an in-depth analysis of the funding items identified in the planning stage. Here an understanding of any current systems needs to be obtained including what will happen to those systems and if they are to be replaced (e.g. how that will be managed).

- **Design:** Here the outputs of the Financial Management implementation are described and designed. Processes are identified as well as valuation models and chargeback methods. All of the procedures, together with roles and responsibilities, will need to be designed at this stage.

- **Implement:** This is where the planned processes are made operational.
- **Measure:** Measures of success will be required and should have been agreed at the planning stage. Auditing will provide assurance that processes are being adhered to.

13 BUSINESS RELATIONSHIP MANAGER

INTRODUCTION

A Business Relationship Manager needs to have an in-depth understanding of the business area they are responsible for.

BUSINESS RELATIONSHIP MANAGEMENT

The Process or Function responsible for maintaining a relationship with the business. Business Relationship Management usually includes:

- managing personal relationships with Business Managers;
- providing input to Service Portfolio Management;
- ensuring that the IT Service Provider is satisfying the business needs of the customers.

This Process has strong links with Service Level Management.

Business Relationship Management centres on maintaining and building the relationship with the business areas.

RELATIONSHIP

A connection or interaction between two people or things. In Business Relationship Management it is the interaction between the IT Service Provider and the business.

There are a number of job titles that are applied to individuals that conduct Business Relationship Management and they vary from organisation to organisation. Examples include Account Managers, Sales Managers and Business Representatives.

THE ROLE

Main book references: SS 4.1.3, 5.5.4.5

Business Relationship Managers are responsible for:

- developing and maintaining a strong business relationship with customers;
- managing customer opportunities through the Service Portfolio;
- liaising with Product Managers who are responsible for developing and managing service across the Lifecycle;
- working closely with Service Level Management to understand the delivery of service and any issues;
- consulting with Financial Management to ensure that financial information is available on the services offered to the business and that the services demonstrate value;
- taking an overview of any complaints and disputes that have come from the business area;
- liaising with other Business Relationship Managers to develop best practice and to propagate that best practice;
- identifying the most appropriate Service Level Package (SLP) for the demands of the business area;
- identifying in consultation with the Product Manager the most appropriate Lines of Service from the Service Catalogue for the business area;
- championing and explaining the activities of the business area within the IT Service Provider;
- championing and explaining the activities of the IT Service Provider within the business area.

14 SOA ROLES AND RESPONSIBILITIES

This chapter sets out the key roles and responsibilities of the Service Catalogue Manager, the Service Level Manager and the Supplier Manager.

SERVICE CATALOGUE MANAGER

Main book reference: SD 6.4.5

The overriding responsibility of the Service Catalogue Manager is the production and revision of the Service Catalogue. It is important that the Service Catalogue is kept up to date.

The Service Catalogue Manager is responsible for the Service Catalogue Management process. They should:

- ensure that all services that are in operation are included in the Service Catalogue;
- ensure that all services intended for operation (moving to transition) are included in the Service Catalogue;
- ensure that Retired Services are removed from the Service Catalogue at the appropriate time;
- ensure that the information and detail held within the Service Catalogue is accurate and current;
- ensure that there is a match between information within the Service Catalogue and information within the Service Portfolio;
- ensure that awareness of the Service Catalogue and its contents is raised both within IT areas and within the business areas.

SERVICE LEVEL MANAGER

Main book reference: SD 6.4.6

The key role of the Service Level Manager is to ensure that the aims of Service Level Management are met.

Responsibilities include:

- ensuring that Service Level Agreements are in place for all services;
- ensuring that all necessary Operational Level Agreements are in place;
- working with Supplier Management in order to ensure that all required Underpinning Contracts are in place;
- discussing and agreeing Service Level Requirements;
- negotiating and agreeing Service Level Agreements;
- negotiating and agreeing Operational Level Agreements;
- liaising closely with the business areas in order to understand their changing needs;
- inputting to the production of the Service Portfolio and the Service Catalogue;
- monitoring and reporting on performance against Service Level Targets;
- undertaking regular Service Reviews;
- identifying opportunities for Continual Service Improvement and managing Service Improvement Plans;
- ensuring all changes are assessed for their likely or potential impact on Service Levels;
- acting as a focal point within the IT Service Provider for issues concerning service;
- acting as a bridge between the IT Service Provider and the business areas;
- developing communications and relationships with key business stakeholders;
- managing complaints that have been escalated;
- measuring and improving customer satisfaction.

SUPPLIER MANAGER

Main book reference: SD 6.4.11

The key role of the Supplier Manager is to ensure that the aims of Supplier Management are met.

Responsibilities include:

- managing suppliers;
- managing contracts;
- maintaining the Supplier and Contracts Database;
- undertaking regular contract reviews;
- monitoring and reporting on supplier performance;

- building and developing relationships with suppliers;
- undertaking regular risk analysis on all suppliers and contracts;
- ensuring that contract targets align to Service Level Targets;
- ensuring value for money is obtained from all suppliers and all contracts;
- ensuring that any dependencies between different suppliers for the delivery of a service are documented and understood;
- updating contracts under Change Control;
- maintaining and managing a process to cater for contractual disputes;
- ensuring that there is a process in place to cater for the renewal of contracts;
- ensuring that there is a process in place to cater for the termination of contracts;
- ensuring all relevant changes are assessed for their likely or potential impact on contracts.

15 TECHNOLOGY AND IMPLEMENTATION CONSIDERATIONS

This chapter looks at the generic requirements and evaluation criteria for technology as well as good practices for process implementation.

GENERIC REQUIREMENTS TO ASSIST SERVICE DESIGN

Main book reference: SD 7.1

There are a multitude of tools that can be used to aid the design of services. Tools exist that can help with the hardware design, software design, process design, data design and environmental design. Some tools are enablers allowing something to happen, while others speed up the design process. There are also tools that ensure standards and conventions are adhered to and others that validate designs.

It can be very useful to have a graphical view of a service as it evolves, detailing the underpinning components and infrastructure and hopefully showing the links to the business processes. This allows dependencies to be quickly identified and their implications managed. It is also something that is meaningful to the business areas who are to be the recipients of the service.

A tool that can provide the end-to-end graphical view, coupled with links to the financial information including the cost of each component, is very powerful. Such tools can be used throughout the organisation in order to support:

- management of all stages of the Service Lifecycle;
- all aspects of service delivery;
- all aspects of service performance;
- provision of metrics and Key Performance Indicators;
- consistency of approach across services;
- management of costs;
- management of relationships and dependencies.

EVALUATION CRITERIA FOR PROCESS IMPLEMENTATION

Main book reference: SD 7.2

The aim of evaluation is to ensure that the correct decision is made for the organisation with regard to the procurement of tools. The tools are intended to make Service Design more effective and efficient and this must drive the decision-making process.

There are a number of areas that need to be taken into account, including:

- Functionality
- Cost
- Usability
- Integration
- Conformance to standards
- Flexibility
- Support
- Scalability
- Tool credibility
- Vendor credibility
- Ease of implementation

A Statement of Requirements should be drawn up. Chapter 11 on Supplier Management covers this. The process for procuring a tool will be the same as procuring any other service or asset. In the Statement of Requirements, the tool requirements should be ranked in terms of 'MUST have', 'SHOULD have', 'COULD have' and 'WON'T have now, but WOULD like in the future'.

The alternative options can then be measured against the Statement of Requirements and a decision can be made. All the 'MUST' or mandatory requirements have to be met. Ease of implementation is important to assess. Time and cost will be saved if the tool needs little or no configuration or customisation, and can be implemented 'out of the box'. Increasing amounts of configuration and customisation will have implications for cost, time, support, training, scalability etc.

GOOD PRACTICE

Main book references: SD 8.2, 8.3, 8.4

The implementation of Service Design must take into account the environment into which it is being introduced. The normal day-to-day operations of the organisation must not be adversely impacted. Any adverse impact at this stage will create a communication and credibility issue for the ongoing practice or process.

In order to obtain the full benefit of implementing IT Service Management, all the processes should be put in place. However, this is not always possible at the outset. Where it is not possible, all areas need to be considered in order to ascertain the areas of greatest need: in other words, what is hurting the organisation most? Quick wins should be identified and implemented. This has the benefit of gaining credibility for the overall implementation in the early days of the process. Care should be exercised to ensure quick wins align to the strategic direction agreed and that they will not cost more in the long term. The implementation should be conducted using a structured project management method.

The implementation cycle is very helpful for tracking progress and ensuring that there is an alignment between IT and the business areas. This cycle can also be used for improving services or processes.

The cycle consists of the following questions that need answering:

1 What is the vision? – high-level business objectives

2 Where are we now? – assessments and benchmarks

3 Where do we want to be? – measurable targets

4 How do we get there? – process improvement

5 How can we tell we have got there? – measurements and metrics (agreed at the outset)

6 How do we keep going? – the cycle then loops back to the start

CHALLENGES, CRITICAL SUCCESS FACTORS AND RISKS

Main book references: ST 9.1–9.3, SO 9.1–9.3, SD 9.1, 9.2

The challenges that may be encountered when implementing new practices or processes are:

- having to align with existing infrastructure and processes;
- a lack of awareness of business requirements;
- gaining management commitment;
- obtaining funding and resources;
- preventing resources from being over committed and being pulled into business-as-usual activity;
- developing mature supporting processes;
- gaining the support of external suppliers;
- overcoming resistance to change and inertia within the organisation;
- finding justification and identifying a return on investment;
- a lack of communication between the IT Service Provider and the business areas;

- a lack of communication within the IT Service Provider;
- a lack of communication within the business areas;
- breaking down the 'stovepipes' that exist within both the IT Service Provider and within the business areas;
- attempting to make improvements without a clear strategy leading to tactical rather than strategic solutions;
- a lack of information, monitoring and measurements;
- using poor or inadequate toolsets.

These challenges can be tackled and overcome by understanding how the business works and its requirements, by involving key stakeholders, by proactive communication and by gaining the support and sponsorship of senior management.

The Critical Success Factors that are relevant for the implementation of practices and processes include:

- assignment of clear process ownership;
- clear objectives and procedures;
- business buy-in;
- senior management support;
- provision of adequate staff;
- provision of adequate funding;
- provision of training for staff and users;
- retention of key staff;
- effective tool support.

Risks that need to be identified and managed include:

- if the maturity level of one process is low, it will not be possible to attain full maturity in other processes – the one process will act as the lowest common denominator dragging the other processes down;
- unrealistic expectations and timescales;
- unclear business requirements and lack of business support;
- insufficient resources;
- a lack of management support;
- a lack of a shared vision across the IT Service Provider in relation to the paradigm shift required to move towards service-focused delivery;
- processes being implemented in isolation without integration – this could cause new 'stovepipes' to form, which is to be avoided.

PLANNING AND IMPLEMENTATION

Main book reference: SO 8.5

There are five key areas that require planning with regard to the implementation of Service Management technologies:

- **Licences:** The cost of tools is often determined by the number of licences required. A form of demand planning is undertaken in order to ascertain the most efficient and effective way to use the tool and to understand how many concurrent users are forecast. Licences may be dedicated or shared. Increasingly 'service on demand' is provided, where access is given for the period of demand and then removed when the demand declines.

- **Deployment:** It will need to be ascertained early in the process whether physical deployment is required or whether the new tool or functionality can be distributed via the network. The number of locations is obviously a vital input to the deployment planning.

- **Capacity checks:** These ensure there is enough capacity for the new tool and its deployment. Importantly, the impact on the capacity of other tools and operations needs to be considered: there are many examples of much heralded successful implementations that thereafter cause degraded service elsewhere within the infrastructure.

- **Timing of technology deployment:** The timing must be appropriate to the organisation's level of IT Service Management maturity. Training and awareness must be coordinated and managed as part of the deployment.

- **Type of introduction:** A decision needs to be taken on whether a phased or a 'big bang' (with perhaps a period of parallel running) approach is most appropriate.

SECTION 3:
PASSING THE SOA EXAMINATION

16 THE SCOPE OF THE EXAM AND THE QUALIFICATION

INTRODUCTION

The purpose of this section of the book is to improve your ability to pass the examination by making sure that you are properly prepared, understand how the examination is structured and know what is expected of you. Although you obviously need an understanding of the subject matter, knowing how the questions are formatted will help to ensure that you are not taken by surprise when you first turn over your examination paper. Also, at the Intermediate level, you are not being tested simply on your knowledge of the subject, but also on your ability to use that knowledge to, for example, analyse information and then make a correct decision based on that analysis.

The better prepared you are for the examination, the more likely you are to pass it. Furthermore, this preparation is equally valid for all of the other Intermediate exams, both the Capability modules and the Lifecycle modules. The same insight will therefore serve you well as you extend your expertise and follow the route towards the expert and master level, if that is your aim.

The following boxed areas on Target Candidate Group, Learning Objectives, Prerequisite Entry Criteria, Eligibility for Examination and Bloom's Taxonomy are taken more or less directly from the Service Offerings and Agreements Certificate Syllabus published by the APM Group. It is important to read through these areas as a reminder of the scope and intention of the exam and certificate.

TARGET CANDIDATE GROUP

The target group for the ITIL Certificate in Service Offerings and Agreements is:

- individuals who have attained the V3 ITIL Foundation Certificate in Service Management or the V3 Foundation Bridge Certificate and who wish to advance to higher ITIL certifications;

- individuals who require a deep understanding of the ITIL Certificate in Service Offerings and Agreements processes and how they may be used to enhance the quality of IT Service Management within an organisation;

- IT professionals that are working in an organisation that has adopted ITIL who need to be informed about and thereafter contribute to an ongoing Service improvement programme;

- Operational staff involved in Service Portfolio Management, Service Catalogue Management, Service Level Management, Demand Management, Supplier Management, Financial Management and Business Relationship Management who wish to enhance their role-based capabilities.

This may include, but is not limited to, IT professionals, Business Managers and Business Process Owners.

LEARNING OBJECTIVES

Candidates can expect to gain competencies in the following areas on completion of the education and examination components related to this certification:

- Service Management as a Practice.

- Processes across the Service Lifecycle pertaining to the Service Offerings and Agreements curriculum.

- Service Portfolio Management which provides documentation for services and prospective services in business terms.

- Service Catalogue Management which is concerned with the production and documentation of the Service Catalogue from a business and a technical viewpoint.

- Service Level Management which sets up a Service Level Agreement (SLA) structure and ensures that all SLAs have an underpinning support structure in place.

- Demand Management which identifies Patterns of Business Activity to enable the appropriate strategy to be implemented.

- Supplier Management which ensures all partners and suppliers are managed in the appropriate way and includes contract management.

- Financial Management which includes ensuring understanding of the service value and the management of all financial considerations.

- Business Relationship Managers who have responsibility to represent customers and ensure the Service Catalogue and Portfolio respond to the needs of the business.

- Operational activities of processes covered in other Lifecycle phases such as Incident and Change Management.

- Organising for Service Offerings and Agreements which describes functions to be performed within Service Offerings and Agreements.

- Service Offerings and Agreements roles and responsibilities.

- Technology and Implementation Considerations.

- Challenges, Critical Success Factors and Risks.
- Continual Service Improvement as a consequence of effective Service Offerings and Agreements.

PREREQUISITE ENTRY CRITERIA

Candidates wishing to be trained and examined for this qualification must already hold the ITIL Foundation Certificate in IT Service Management (the V3 Foundation or V2 Foundation plus Bridge Certificate) which needs to be presented as documentary evidence to gain admission to the training and exam.

It is also strongly recommended that candidates:

- can demonstrate familiarity with IT terminology and understand the context of Service Offerings and Agreements in their own business environment;
- have exposure working in a Service Management capacity within a Service Provider environment, with responsibility which incorporates at least one of the following Service Management processes:

  o Service Portfolio Management
  o Service Catalogue Management
  o Service Level Management
  o Demand Management
  o Supplier Management
  o Financial Management

It is recommended that candidates are familiar with the guidance detailed in the ITIL Service Lifecycle core publications prior to attending training for this certification.

ELIGIBILITY FOR EXAMINATION

The candidate must fill the following requirements to be eligible for the examination leading to an accredited ITIL Certificate in Service Offerings and Agreements:

- At least 30 contact hours training (hours of instruction, excluding breaks, with an Accredited Training Organisation (ATO) or an accredited e-learning solution) for the Service Offerings and Agreements syllabus, as part of a formal, approved training course/scheme.
- There is no minimum mandatory requirement, but two to four years professional experience working in IT Service Management is highly desirable.
- Hold the ITIL V3 Foundation Certificate in IT Service Management or ITIL V2 Foundation plus the bridging certificate.

> • It is also recommended that candidates should complete at a minimum twelve hours of personal study by reviewing the syllabus and the pertinent areas of the ITIL Service Management core guidance publications and in particular the Service Strategy and Service Design publications.

BLOOM'S TAXONOMY AND ITS USE IN THE TRAINING AND EXAMINATION

All ITIL Service Management certifications use Bloom's taxonomy in both the construction of the learning units and in the examination which is based on the syllabus.

A learning taxonomy is a scale of the degree of difficulty in the learning process. These levels apply to the cognitive, affective and psychomotor domains of learning, but in the ITIL Qualification Scheme, only the cognitive sphere is included.

Benjamin S Bloom (1913–99) was an American Educational Psychologist who studied educational objectives. In 1956 he published his work *Taxonomy of Educational Objectives Handbook 1: Cognitive Domain.* 'Taxonomy' simply means 'classification', which for students of the ITIL exams means a classification of types and levels of IT Service Management learning. The 'Cognitive Domain' encompasses knowledge structures at six levels.

These six levels of learning are both sequential and cumulative. They move from the simple to the complex. This implies that in order to achieve the sixth level of learning, for example, the instructor must ensure that the previous five levels have been mastered. For the Service Offerings and Agreement exam, mastery of levels 1–4 is required. This should be acquired through a balance of knowledge, experience, training and study.

The six levels, stages or phases are defined below. The work undertaken by Bloom was added to in 2001 by Anderson and Krathwohl. They used equivalent levels for the four Bloom levels relevant to this exam with alternative names (shown in brackets).

- **Level 1 Knowledge (Remembering):** Here the student is able to bring to mind or remember the appropriate material. The behavioural tasks associated with this level tax the student's memory and include such tasks as defining, recalling, listing, recognising, describing and naming.

- **Level 2 Comprehension (Understanding):** Here the student is able to understand or grasp the meaning of what is being communicated and make use of the idea without relating it to other ideas or materials and without seeing the fullest possible meaning or translation of the idea. Behavioural tasks at this level would include stating in the student's own words, giving examples of, illustrating, inferring, summarising and interpreting. These actions involve the knowing which has taken place at the first level.

- **Level 3 Application (Applying):** Here the student should be able to use ideas, principles and theories in new, particular and concrete situations.

Behavioural tasks at this level involve both knowing and comprehension and might include choosing appropriate procedures, applying principles, using an approach or identifying the selection of options.

- **Level 4 Analysis (Analysing):** At this level the student is able to break down a communication (rendered in any form) into constituent parts in order to make the organisation and significance of the whole clear. Breaking down, discriminating, diagramming, detecting, differentiating and illustrating are important behavioural tasks at this level and can be seen to include the previous levels of knowing, comprehending and applying. Here the significance of the constituent parts of an entity are examined in order to understand the whole more fully.

- **Level 5 Synthesis:** At this level (mastery of which is not required by the SOA exam), the student is able to put back together the various parts or elements of a concept into a unified organisation or whole. This process, together with making sense of small parts, is a crucial factor in intelligence and learning. Behavioural tasks at this level would include creating, writing, designing, combining, composing, organising, revising and planning. This level of learning in order to occur must include the first four levels. It is probably the most intense and exciting level for student and teacher alike.

- **Level 6 Evaluation:** In this phase (mastery of which is not required by the SOA exam), the student is able to arrive at an overview and to judge the value and relative merit of ideas or procedures by using appropriate criteria. At this level of learning the student will be able to compare, judge, appraise, justify, criticise and contrast theories, procedures, methods and concepts. This level involves mastery of the five previous levels.

Intermediate ITIL qualifications, such as Service Offerings and Agreements, will examine according to Bloom's Levels 1–4 with the appropriate level assigned to each syllabus unit. This means that the candidate must be prepared to be tested up to and including Level 4 for any question relating to that learning unit or units. In other words, for the six key processes of Service Offerings and Agreements (i.e. Service Portfolio Management, Service Catalogue Management, Service Level Management, Supplier Management, Demand Management and Financial Management), the candidate needs to be prepared to be tested at the knowing, comprehending, applying and analysing levels.

17 TRAINING

INTRODUCTION

This chapter looks at the obligatory formal classroom or e-learning training where you will study the subject matter in some detail using a combination of approaches. Examination candidates may already be familiar with some aspects of the syllabus; however, the study time is crucial because it will allow all the topics to be covered as a whole, including how they all fit together. Preparation time will also include looking at sample papers and gaining an understanding of what to expect in the exam.

The formal training you receive may be a public course where the attendees come from a variety of different organisations or it may be an in-house course with a group of other people from the same organisation. The former provides an opportunity to compare and contrast different approaches taken by the organisations represented. It is always interesting to hear where other organisations are in terms of their Service Management journey. In-house courses allow in-depth discussion and analysis of the processes in the way that they are relevant to their organisation.

TRAINING, DURATION, STRUCTURE AND CONTENT

The course typically lasts five days with the examination on the afternoon of the fifth day. Courses are often residential, but this varies from course to course. Training comprises a combination of tutor presentation, classroom discussion, exercises to reinforce the learning and sample papers.

Different people will absorb information and ideas in different ways. It is important to understand what works best for each individual. Reading and listening alone are often not sufficient to gain a full understanding. Course attendees and exam candidates will be encouraged to discuss and challenge the material. This is important because the examination is at Bloom's Level 4, which requires the candidates to be able to remember, understand, apply and analyse the subject matter included within the syllabus.

The syllabus is detailed in Appendix 1, but, in summary, the topics you will cover and the time allocated to each are shown in Figure 17.1.

Figure 17.1 Syllabus topics and study hours

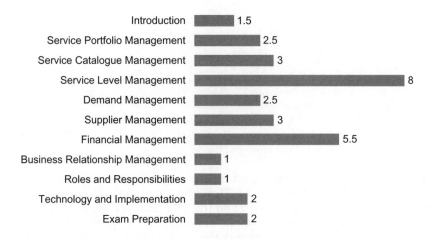

The order in which the subjects are covered is not set. However, there is a logical flow to covering them in the order suggested in the diagram.

18 THE FORMAT OF THE EXAMINATION

INTRODUCTION

The format of the exam and the structure of the questions is different to many exams and certainly different to the ITIL V3 Foundation Certificate in IT Service Management or ITIL V2 Foundation and the V3 bridging certificate. Therefore, it is important that time on the course and subsequently is spent on looking at sample questions. This will save time in the exam proper and avoid confusion as to what is required. For this purpose four sample exam questions are presented in Appendix 2, with the answers and the rationale.

Candidates can sit an Intermediate exam for the first time only as part of an accredited training course. If a candidate fails the examination, they may resit it by joining another invigilated examination at the end of an accredited course without attending the training. Candidates do not need to join another SOA course, but can sit the SOA examination on any other invigilated course with the permission of the trainer(s) and the accredited training provider, and by prior submission to the relevant examination board (this is normally done on the candidate's behalf by the training provider).

The time allowed for the examination is 90 minutes. The examination paper comprises eight questions, all of which should be attempted. Eight questions in 90 minutes allows, on average, ten minutes per question plus ten minutes' checking time at the end. Candidates who are sitting the exam in a language other than their first language are allowed 120 minutes and are allowed to use a dictionary.

FORMAT OF THE QUESTIONS

All Intermediate examinations, including Service Offerings and Agreements, use scenario-based questions that are gradient scored. Each question consists of a short (up to 400 words) scenario or case study, a question statement and four possible answers. Candidates are expected to be able to correctly answer the questions based on leading practices included within the ITIL core books (principally Service Strategy and Service Design for the SOA examination) together with the knowledge and experience expected of those who meet the prerequisite entry criteria. Candidates are not expected to memorise minor details from the core books.

Of the four possible answers to each question, one is considered to be the most correct or best answer and is worth 5 marks. Another answer is the second or next best response and is worth 3 marks. Another answer is the third best response and receives 1 mark and the remaining answer is the least correct response and is sometimes referred to as a 'Distracter'. The least correct response receives no marks. There are no negative marks or marks deducted for selecting particular answers.

Question compilers, and those who provide quality assurance for examination questions, have guidelines for question setting that include:

- answers should not be distinguished by very small differences in wording;
- questions should neither assume a prior knowledge of ITIL V2 nor the distinctions between V2 and V3;
- questions should not ask for an opinion, but in the circumstances of the case study or scenario, which answer provides the correct or best option.

Within the paper, two questions may share the same scenario, although it will be repeated in the question paper for each question and will be on a different learning unit.

Questions may cover multiple learning units (see Appendix 1) or, more typically, single learning units. The will be a balance of learning units tested across the eight questions, but with ten learning units in total, not all will be represented in any one examination paper. There will be no more than two questions on any one learning unit.

THE EXAMINATION ENVIRONMENT

You will normally sit the examination in the same room in which the training took place. The examination will be on the afternoon of the last day of the course. Using the same room gives some familiarity and allows any issues concerning temperature or noise to be identified.

The examination will be overseen by an invigilator. The trainer usually leaves the room and the invigilator takes over.

Before the examination starts, it is preferable that the trainer arranges the room to meet the invigilator's requirements. This means arranging the seating far enough apart to avoid the possibility of copying and, since this is a closed book examination, removing all references to the course and syllabus material that may be on the wall, on whiteboards or flip charts. All loose paper, textbooks and sample papers will likewise be removed.

Ideally, the trainer or invigilator will ensure that candidates are not disturbed by noise from adjacent rooms by advising all relevant people that an examination is taking place. External noise should be minimised by shutting windows. No personal music players are allowed and there will be strictly no talking.

Candidates may take a drink into the examination, but this should be organised prior to the start of the exam.

You should complete the examination grid in pencil. Pencils will be provided by the invigilator. A clock should be made available, but regardless of whether or not one is in place, the invigilator will remind candidates of the time gone or outstanding time at regular intervals during the 90 minutes. There will be a verbal warning from the invigilator when there is five minutes to go before the end of the examination.

During their introduction, the invigilator will cover the basics of the exam and what is expected. These include provision for a comfort break and leaving before the 90 minutes has expired. Apart from in the last 15 minutes, most invigilators will allow candidates to leave as long as they can exit the room without disturbing other candidates. The best policy is to stay until the end of the exam and ensure that answers have been checked through.

The invigilator will hand out three booklets:

- A scenario booklet containing eight scenarios.
- A question booklet containing the eight questions and the four possible answers for each question.
- An answer booklet in which you can indicate your answer.

Candidates may write on the scenario booklet or the question booklet, but only answers on the answer booklet will be marked. The answer booklet lets you indicate your answer to each question on a grid by shading an answer box. Answer booklets are usually generic and may well have room for more than eight questions. It is important that candidates are aware prior to the start of the examination which boxes need to be completed.

TYPICAL EXAMINATION QUESTION STRUCTURES AND STYLES

All questions in the exam have certain common attributes:

- A scenario, that is some text describing a situation, circumstances, objectives etc. The scenario will normally comprise no more than 400 words.
- A question. The question will normally be quite short, but may be up to 200 words. The total length of the scenario and question combined will not normally exceed 600 words.
- Four possible answers.

The question is usually very simple, for instance, 'Which of the following options is the best approach?' However, it may contain some additional information that needs to be considered with the scenario in order to arrive at the best answer.

Most answers are structured as a set of statements. These may be in the form of a bullet list (slightly easier to understand and answer) or may be a string of sentences within a paragraph. There are typically five or six statements in each answer. Answers may be distinguished from each other by time or priority, for example if the question asks in which sequence you would undertake a set of actions, the candidate will need to select the set that has the most logical sequence.

Alternatively, if the answers simply comprise a series of statements, there are three possible ways to distinguish the answers:

- Each answer may contain an entirely different set of statements.
- Each answer may contain some similar statements but worded slightly differently.
- Each answer may contain some common statements and some different statements.

Sometimes the answer statements are grouped into two or three sections. For instance each answer may include a proposed approach, a metric and a conclusion.

The guidance given to question compilers provides some insight into how questions are worded. As a candidate, it is worth noting:

- Very small differences in wording should not be used to mask significant differences between answers.
- Questions should ask what is the 'Best' or 'Correct' answer rather than what is your opinion.
- Questions should not assume an understanding of ITIL V2.
- The 5-mark answer should be completely correct. The 3-mark answer must be less correct than the 5-mark answer but more correct than the 1-mark answer, which in turn must be more correct than the 0-mark answer. However, the 0-mark answer may in some parts be factually correct.
- It should not be possible to identify the correct answer simply from the structure of the answers. (This includes the relative length of the answers.)
- Key words such as 'BEST', 'MOST', 'CANNOT' and 'PRIMARY' should be capitalised.
- There should be no more than two questions on any one syllabus learning unit, although any question may cover more than one learning unit.
- Two questions may use the same scenario, but should reference different syllabus learning units.

GUIDANCE ON SELECTING THE BEST ANSWER

There are a number of methods of approaching the questions. Reading the question thoroughly is paramount and a methodical approach to selecting the answer is recommended. Candidates should use mock papers to discover which approach works for them.

The step-by-step guide that follows is one approach that reduces the risk of selecting the wrong answer and boosts the candidate's chances of selecting the best answer.

- **Step 1 Manage your time effectively:** Ensure that there is enough time available to properly assess and answer each question.

- **Step 2 Highlight key scenario and question words and statements:** Key words in the scenario or in the question will give an indication of what the question is driving at.

- **Step 3 Eliminate 'noise' from the answers:** Eliminate anything that is not relevant or which is repeated in all four answers.

- **Step 4 Identify key answer statement differences:** Where a statement is repeated in two or more answers with slight differences in wording, this will probably be relevant to the answering of the question.

- **Step 5 Qualify each answer and identify the distracter:** Identifying the distracter or 0-mark answer is very useful. In order to check the logic of selecting a particular answer, attempt to identify which answers are the 5-, 3-, 1- and 0-mark responses.

- **Step 6 Select the answer:** Finalise your decision.

- **Step 7 Check answers:** Check all answers.

In order to pass the exam, candidates must gain 28 marks or more out of a possible 40 (70 per cent or more). This means that five or more of your answers must be the best or second best responses.

APPENDICES

APPENDIX 1
SERVICE OFFERINGS AND AGREEMENTS SYLLABUS

The following is extracted directly from Service Offerings and Agreements Certificate Syllabus published by the APM Group. It shows the scope of the learning needed to pass the examination and the Bloom's level of difficulty for each module that will be tested in the examination. Candidates will notice that apart from Unit 1, all Units have a Bloom's level of 4.

The ITIL Intermediate Qualification: Service Offerings and Agreements is awarded to those who complete the following units of study and successfully pass the relevant examination. The units cover the topics listed (section numbers from the source publications are included along with indicative contact study hours).

UNIT 1 INTRODUCTION

Level of difficulty: Up to Bloom's level 2

This unit introduces the candidate to the concepts and terminology of the Service Lifecycle and the role of SOA within the Lifecycle.

To meet the learning outcomes and examination level of difficulty, the candidates must be able to understand and describe:

- the concept of Service Management as a practice (SS 2.1, ST 2.1);
- the concept of Service, its value proposition and composition (SS 2.2, ST 2.2);
- the functions and process across the Lifecycle (SS 2.6, ST 2.3);
- the role of Processes in the Service Lifecycle (SS 2.6.2, SS 2.6.3);
- how Service Management creates business value (SS 3.1, SD 2.4.3, ST 2.4.3, SO 2.4.3, CSI 3.7.2);
- how the processes within the Service Offerings and Agreement curriculum supports the Service Lifecycle (SD 2.4.5, SS 5.1 up to 5.1.2, SS 5.5.1, SS 5.3 up to 5.3.1).

The recommended minimum study period for this unit is 1.5 hours.

UNIT 2 SERVICE PORTFOLIO MANAGEMENT

Level of difficulty: Up to Bloom's level 4

This unit covers the Service Portfolio Management process and how it contributes to Service Offerings and Agreements.

To meet the learning outcomes and examination level of difficulty, the candidates must be able to understand, describe, identify, demonstrate, apply, distinguish, produce, decide or analyse:

- the Service Portfolio and illustrate its relationship with the Service Catalogue and Service Pipeline (SS 4.2.3, SS 5.1.2.3);
- how a Service Portfolio describes a provider's service and how it relates the business service with the IT service (SS 5.3);
- the Service Portfolio Management methods (SS 5.4).

The recommended minimum study period for this unit is 2.5 hours.

UNIT 3 SERVICE CATALOGUE MANAGEMENT

Level of difficulty: Up to Bloom's level 4

This unit covers the Service Catalogue Management process and how it is integrated with the Service Portfolio.

To meet the learning outcomes and examination level of difficulty, the candidates must be able to understand, describe, identify, demonstrate, apply, distinguish, produce, decide or analyse:

- the purpose, goal and objectives of the process (SD 4.1.1);
- the scope of the process (SD 4.1.2);
- the interface to the Service Portfolio (SS 4.2.3, SD 3.6.2, SD 3.9, SD 3.10);
- the difference between a Business and a Technical Service Catalogue (SD 4.1.4);
- the importance of the Service Catalogue to the Service Lifecycle and the business (SS 4.2.3, SD 3.10, SD 4.1.3);
- its policies, principles and basic concepts (SD 4.1.4);
- the use of key metrics, challenges, critical success factors and risks associated with the process (SD 4.1.8, SD 4.1.9);
- the process including the utilisation of the Service Catalogue by other processes and functions (SD 4.1.5, SD 4.1.6);
- produce a Service Catalogue (SD Appendix G).

The recommended minimum study period for this unit is 3.0 hours.

UNIT 4 SERVICE LEVEL MANAGEMENT

Level of difficulty: Up to Bloom's level 4

This unit covers the Service Level Management process and deliverables.

To meet the learning outcomes and examination level of difficulty, the candidates must be able to understand, describe, identify, demonstrate, apply, distinguish, produce, decide or analyse:

- the purpose, goal and objectives of the SLM (SD 4.2.1);
- the scope of the SLM (SD 4.2.2);
- the importance of the process to the Service Lifecycle and how it generates business value (SD 4.2 up to 4.2.1, SD 4.2.3);
- the principles and basic concepts (SD 4.2.4);
- the main activities, methods and techniques of this process and how it relates to the Service Lifecycle – this includes the SLA structures and determining Service Level Requirements (SD 4.2.5 up to 4.2.5.3 including figures 4.5, 4.6 and 4.7);
- the deliverables from the process (SD 4.2.5.6, SD 4.2.5.7);
- monitoring of service performance against SLAs (SD 4.2.5.3, CSI 3.5);
- the use of key metrics, challenges, critical success factors and risks associated with the process (SD 4.2.7, SD 4.2.8, SD 4.2.9);
- the contents of SLAs, OLAs and review meetings (SD 4.2.5.5, SD 4.2.5.8, SD Appendix F);
- the interfaces to other processes and functions (SD 4.2.5 up to 4.2.5.1, figure 4.5, SD 4.2.5.4,, SD 4.2.5.8, SD 4.2.5.9, SD 4.2.6).

The recommended minimum study period for this unit is 8.0 hours.

UNIT 5 DEMAND MANAGEMENT

Level of difficulty: Up to Bloom's level 4

This unit covers the Demand Management process and how it contributes to Service Offerings and Agreements.

To meet the learning outcomes and examination level of difficulty, the candidates must be able to understand, describe, identify, demonstrate, apply, distinguish, produce, decide or analyse:

- the basic concepts of the process (SS 5.5.1);
- activity-based Demand Management and business activity patterns (SS 5.5.2, SS 5.5.3, SS figure 5.23);

- the interfaces to Service Portfolio (SS 5.5.2);
- managing demand for Service (SS 5.5.3, table 5.8, table 5.9).

The recommended minimum study period for this unit is 2.5 hours.

UNIT 6 SUPPLIER MANAGEMENT

Level of difficulty: Up to Bloom's level 4

This unit covers the use of the Supplier Management process and the interfaces and dependencies of the process.

To meet the learning outcomes and examination level of difficulty, the candidates must be able to understand, describe, identify, demonstrate, apply, distinguish, produce, decide or analyse:

- the purpose, goal and objectives of the process (SD 4.7.1);
- the scope of the process (SD 4.7.2);
- the importance of the process to the Service Lifecycle and how they generate business value (SD 4.7.3);
- the principles and basic concepts (SD 4.7.4);
- the main activities, methods and techniques of this process and how it relates to the Service Lifecycle including evaluation of new suppliers (SD 4.7.5 up to 4.7.5.2, SD 4.7.5.3, SD 4.7.5.4, SD 4.7.5.5);
- the use of Supplier Categorisation and maintenance of the Supplier Database (SD 4.7.5.2);
- the use of key metrics, challenges, critical success factors and risks associated with the process (SD 4.7.7, SD 4.7.9);
- the inputs and outputs of the process (SD 4.7.6).

The recommended minimum study period for this unit is 3.0 hours.

UNIT 7 FINANCIAL MANAGEMENT

Level of difficulty: Up to Bloom's level 4

This unit covers how Financial Management contributes to the Service Lifecycle Operation and the basic principles of Service Economics.

To meet the learning outcomes and examination level of difficulty, the candidates must be able to understand, describe, identify, demonstrate, apply, distinguish, produce, decide or analyse:

- the purpose, goal and objectives of the process (SS 5.1 up to 5.1.2);
- the scope of the process (SS 5.1.2 up to 5.1.2.1);

- the concepts of Service Valuation (SS 5.1.2.1, SS 5.1.3.1, SS figure 5.3);
- the importance of the process to the Service Lifecycle and how they generate business value (SS 5.1 opening section, SS 5.1.1);
- the various aspects of the process and the basic concepts – funding, accounting and chargeback (SS 5.1.2.5, SS 5.1.2.6, SS 5.1.2.7, SS 5.1.4.2);
- Return on Investment and the business case (SS 5.2 up to 5.2.2.1, SS 5.2.3 up to 5.2.3.1);
- the main activities, methods and techniques that enable this process and how it relates to the Service Lifecycle (SS 5.1.3);
- Design and Implement a Financial Management process (SS 5.1.4.3);

The recommended minimum study period for this unit is 5.5 hours.

UNIT 8 BUSINESS RELATIONSHIP MANAGER

Level of difficulty: Up to Bloom's level 4

This unit covers the role of Business Relationship Manager.

To meet the learning outcomes and examination level of difficulty, the candidates must be able to understand, describe, identify, demonstrate, apply, distinguish, produce, decide or analyse:

- the role of Business Relationship Managers (SS 4.1.3; SS 5.5.4.5).

The recommended minimum study period for this unit is 1.0 hours.

UNIT 9 SERVICE OFFERINGS AND AGREEMENT ROLES AND RESPONSIBILITIES

Level of difficulty: Up to Bloom's level 4

This unit covers how Service roles and responsibilities contribute to Service Offerings and Agreement.

To meet the learning outcomes and examination level of difficulty, the candidates must be able to understand, describe, identify, demonstrate, apply, distinguish, produce, decide or analyse:

- key roles and responsibilities of the Service Catalogue Manager (SD 6.4.5);
- key roles and responsibilities of the Service Level Manager (SD 6.4.6);
- key roles and responsibilities pertaining to the Supplier Manager (SD 6.4.11).

The recommended minimum study period for this unit is 1.0 hours.

UNIT 10 TECHNOLOGY AND IMPLEMENTATION CONSIDERATIONS

Level of difficulty: Up to Bloom's level 4

This unit covers technology implementation as part of implementing service management process capabilities, and what special technology functions and features are related to Service Offerings and Agreement practices.

To meet the learning outcomes and examination level of difficulty, the candidates must be able to understand, describe, identify, demonstrate, apply, distinguish, produce, decide or analyse:

- the generic requirements for technology to assist Service Design (SD 7.1);
- the evaluation criteria for technology and tooling for process implementation (SD 7.2);
- the good practices for practice and process implementation (SD 8.2, 8.3, 8.4);
- the challenges, Critical Success Factors and risks related to implementing practices and processes (ST 9.1–9.3, SO 9.1–9.3, SD 9.1–9.2);
- how to plan and implement Service Management technologies (SO 8.5).

The recommended minimum study period for this unit is 2.0 hours.

UNIT 11 SUMMARY, EXAM PREPARATION AND DIRECTED STUDIES

This unit summarises the material covered in the previous units and prepares candidates for the examination. It is likely that most course providers will wish to offer and review at least one mock examination opportunity.

The recommended minimum study period for this unit is 2.0 hours.

APPENDIX 2
SAMPLE QUESTIONS

All questions are version 4.1.

Scenario 1

A financial services organisation has developed a comprehensive portfolio of financial products and services which they offer across North America. Plans are underway to add new products and to expand the operation to include new offices in Europe, the Middle East and the Far East. This expansion will take place over the next two years.

The Business senior management has briefed the Chief Information Officer (CIO) on the expansion plans and has stated that the success of expansion is critically tied to improved IT service performance. The Management has been complaining for the past few months that the quality of IT service performance has been very poor and the issues must be rectified immediately so IT can assure its service warranty meets Business needs as expansion occurs.

The CIO is aware that the major source of this poor service performance is caused by limitations within the international corporate network provided by their network Supplier. Many discussions have taken place with the Supplier to resolve this situation, but there has been no improvement in the performance of the network.

The Supplier has also been slow to react and implement new network connections and facilities within the required timescales and they have also expressed concern that they will be unable to provide the required connectivity and functionality for the new offices in Europe, the Middle East and the Far East.

The decision to replace the network Supplier has been taken by IT and approved by the CIO and the Board.

QUESTION 1

You are an external consultant and have been asked by the Chief Information Officer (CIO) to help evaluate possible Suppliers that can resolve the network issues and restore the IT organisation's reputation with the Business.

When considering Suppliers, which one of the following options is the BEST one to ensure that network issues are addressed to meet the needs of the financial services organisation?

A Consideration should be given to network services being sourced from a single Supplier with a good track record and the ability to deliver products as stipulated within the contract. A list of preferred Suppliers should be drawn up to reduce risk to the organisation and credit checks carried out. There should be good lines of communication and a means of escalation agreed with the Supplier. Service reviews should be held on a regular basis and the cost of service provision clearly agreed, together with service penalty payments. The Supplier should conform to the processes and procedures of the financial services organisation and any sub-contracted work must be agreed by the organisation, with the responsibility resting with the Supplier providing the network service.

B Consideration should be given to engaging two or more competing Suppliers to ensure that quality network services can be obtained at a competitive price and agreed service levels maintained. A list of preferred Suppliers should be drawn up to reduce risk to the organisation and credit checks carried out. The network service offerings of each Supplier should be reviewed for completeness, capability, quality and cost, against the requirements of the financial services organisation. The track record of each company should be verified ensuring that they have the ability to deliver the appropriate network service to the financial services organisation. All identified Suppliers should conform to the financial services organisation's processes and procedures and any sub-contracted work, agreed by the organisation. Responsibility of sub-contracted services must rest with the Supplier providing the service.

C Consideration should be given to entering into a partnership with Suppliers where mutual trust and a good relationship can be established. A list of preferred Suppliers should be drawn up to reduce risk to the organisation and credit checks and references should be completed. The network service offerings should be reviewed for completeness, capability, quality and cost against the requirements of the financial services organisation. There should be a close integration of processes, values and beliefs and the objectives and cultures of the two organisations should be aligned. Communication at all levels should be established with a collective responsibility for service performance and future development. Service performance, costs and risks should be reviewed on a regular basis and agreement reached on how benefits, risks or rewards in terms of material costs are shared.

D Consideration should be given to services being sourced from a single Supplier with a good track record of delivering the network services agreed within the contract. The Contract with the Supplier should stipulate that any increase in service costs should be borne by the supplier to ensure that the financial services organisation can continue to meet its obligations to its customers.

Service reviews should be held on a regular basis to ensure that targets are being met and penalties applied where necessary to ensure that the Supplier delivers on a consistent basis. A credit check should be carried out and references obtained before entering into any formal Contract. The Supplier should conform to the process and procedures of the financial services organisation at all times and any sub-contracted work must be agreed by the financial services organisation.

Scenario 2

A large retailer of fair-trade food products has an internal IT Department running most of its IT operation from the Head Office. There is an intention to manage quality and to maintain and improve the level of the IT service delivered to the Head Office staff and the retail stores. There has been a history of confusion on what is required from the services and what has actually been achieved. This has resulted in a poor relationship between the Business Units and the IT Department.

Some verbal agreements between IT and the Business exist where all levels of response were done on a best endeavour basis. There have been a number of complaints by key staff claiming that the IT staff have been resolving Incidents and implementing Change requests based on operational ease rather than business priority.

A new IT Director has been appointed from an external organisation who has been using the ITIL framework for many years and believes that good IT Service Management practices are essential.

The IT Director is sure that many of the current issues can be rectified through the implementation of Service Level Management (SLM) and has therefore directed that Service Level Agreements are introduced for the services provided before moving onto other areas. You have been asked to lead this project.

QUESTION 2

Which one of the following options is the BEST approach to take?

A   Identify all of the services currently delivered using the Service Catalogue. Meet with the appropriate business representatives and after discussion, document the actual service requirements of the Business in Service Level Agreements (SLAs). Arrange meetings with the IT Design and Operations teams, specifically those involved in Incident, Availability and Capacity Management, to discuss, document and agree the levels of service required. Draft agreements from these discussions are then reviewed by Service Operations to ensure that no existing agreements will be compromised and once this has been confirmed, the SLA is formally agreed and signed. Targets set are then formally monitored, reported on and reviewed at the agreed intervals.

B Identify all the services currently delivered, using the Service Catalogue. Meet with the appropriate business representatives and after discussions produce formal SLAs that document the levels of service that IT can offer. Arrange subsequent meetings with the IT Design and Operations teams, specifically those involved in Incident, Availability and Capacity Management, to discuss and agree the levels of service required. From these discussions Operational Level Agreements (OLAs) are then agreed. These documents can then be signed by IT and all measurements agreed within the document can be formally monitored, reported on and reviewed at the agreed intervals.

C Meet with the IT Operations team; specifically those involved in Incident, Availability and Capacity Management, to define what level of service they can offer the Business. Meet with the appropriate business representatives to give them a clear understanding of the levels of service IT can offer. After negotiation, a draft agreement is produced, formally agreed and signed by representatives of both parties. Confirm with Service Operations that the document will not compromise any existing agreements. Finally, a formal OLA is defined and signed by both the Business and an IT representative. Once this agreement has been signed, all targets within the agreement are then formally monitored, reported on and reviewed at the agreed intervals.

D Identify all of the services currently delivered, using the Service Catalogue. Meet with the appropriate business representatives and after discussion produce a formal SLA that guarantees the levels of service that the Business needs. Subsequent meetings are then arranged with the IT Design and Operations teams, specifically those involved in Incident, Availability and Capacity Management, to inform them of the service levels you have agreed on behalf of IT and start to negotiate the OLAs needed to support these. Once these are agreed and signed the OLAs are passed back to the business to demonstrate that IT will support the SLA and to build on the trust between the two parties.

Scenario 3

You are a Service Management Programme Manager working in a large retail organisation based in Sweden. The Organisation has a reputation for providing high quality products to retail outlets in Europe under its franchise operations. In line with its Business Strategy, it has developed its portfolio of services and products and expanded the operation to include franchise outlets in most European countries. Based on this recent success, the Organisation intends to expand further over the next two years into North America and Asia.

An outcome from a recent meeting of the Board of Directors was that ITIL should be fully adopted by the Organisation with a view to improving the management of IT Services provided to the Business. The Service Level Manager submitted a Service Improvement Programme which has been given outline approval to proceed. It is clear that new, integrated IT Service Management tools are needed that can support the further development and integration of the Service Management processes. The Head of IT understands the value such tools could offer and is supportive of this initiative. The Finance Director however, will not release funds without a formal Business Case being submitted for approval, identifying some of the common business objectives that the tools will address.

QUESTION 3

The Head of IT has asked the Service Level Manager to explain why a Business Case is necessary and what common business objectives would add value to the Business Case.

Which one of the following explanations is BEST?

A A Business Case is essential because it will contain a detailed analysis of the business impact and benefits of the required Service Management tool funding and act as a basis for decision and approval. The impact on the Business can be linked to the business objectives confirming the basis for preparing the business case in the first place.

The common business objectives are:

- an increase in reliability from an operational aspect;
- an improved return on assets from a financial aspect;
- improved customer satisfaction from a strategic aspect.

B A Business Case is essential because it identifies the business requirements that depend on Service Management and will assist the Financial Director in making an informed decision on the Service Management tool costs. This will ensure that appropriate funding is secured for the programme to proceed.

The common business objectives are:

- the introduction of competitive products from an operational aspect;
- improved efficiency from a financial aspect;
- improved customer satisfaction from a financial aspect.

C A Business Case is essential because it identifies the business requirements, the cost of the Service Management tool, the resources required to support the initiative and any risks will be highlighted and known before funding is approved. This will assist the Financial Director in making an informed decision.

The common business objectives are:

- an improvement in resource utilisation from an operational aspect;
- a decrease in non-discretionary spending from a financial aspect;
- an increase in reliability from a strategic aspect.

D A Business Case is essential because it identifies the business requirements that depend on the Service Management tool and will enable the appropriate funding to be secured for the programme to proceed and business objectives will be met.

The common business objectives are:

- better quality from an operational aspect;
- the introduction of competitive products from a financial aspect;
- improved customer satisfaction from a strategic aspect.

Scenario 4

You are the Service Catalogue Manager for a large construction organisation based in New York. Following the recent hostile acquisition of a competitor based in Chicago you have been actioned by Senior Management to review the services that the IT Department in Chicago offers and produce a revised Service Catalogue combining all services provided by both the New York and Chicago locations. It is the intention of the Senior Management team to review what services should be retained, improved or retired.

The New York-based company has good Service Management processes, which have enabled them to produce and maintain up-to-date Business and Technical Service Catalogues. They are willing to cooperate in any way they can.

The Chicago-based organisation have a poor understanding of the services they provide to their customers and do not place any value in the creation of a Service Catalogue because it is seen to be time consuming and a waste of time. Additionally, a blame culture exists within the Business Units and the IT staff in Chicago.

There is strong resistance from the Chicago staff and until now they have been reluctant to assist or provide any information that you have requested.

QUESTION 4

Which one of the following options is the BEST set of actions to take to address the issues identified and produce a revised Service Catalogue?

A • Obtain senior management commitment for support and funding.

• Promote the benefits of Service Catalogue Management (SCM) to the Chicago staff.

• Mount an awareness campaign throughout the organisation and create a joint project.

• Liaise with Service Level Management (SLM) in verifying services and information before adding to the joint Service Catalogue.

• Review processes, tools and resources needed to maintain information.

• Promote the Service Catalogue and maintain it under Change Management.

• Ensure the detail recorded in Service Catalogue is consistent with the Configuration Management System (CMS) and Service Knowledge Management System (SKMS).

• Create meaningful Key Performance Indicators (KPIs) for SCM to measure progress.

B • Obtain Senior Management sponsorship of the project plan.

• Establish a project team with experienced ITIL personnel from both companies.

• Form a project steering group from the management team.

• Use the Service Catalogue from New York and add services once identified.

• Maintain Service Catalogues under Change Management.

• Liaise with SLM in verifying services before adding to the Catalogue.

• Communicate the Service Catalogue and its use throughout the organisation.

• Create meaningful KPIs for SCM.

C • Identify the services used in Chicago and update the Service Catalogue.

• Review incident, problem and change records to extract information about services.

• Liaise with Finance to identify what service invoices have been raised.

• Obtain as much information as possible to enable the Catalogue to be produced.

- Purchase a discovery tool to identify services used in Chicago to enable catalogues to be updated and maintained.

- Review the processes and agree improvements.

- Review tools and resources required to maintain information.

- Publish the revised Service Catalogue on the intranet for internal feedback before it is launched on the Customer web page.

D
- Establish a clear vision for SCM and communicate throughout the organisation.

- Appoint a project manager and team, involving business and IT personnel of both companies.

- Agree the requirements for a Service Catalogue covering services in the merged organisation.

- Review the SCM processes.

- Maintain revised Service Catalogues under Change Management.

- Review the tools and resources required to maintain the information.

- Decide the goals to achieve and the further improvements.

- Create meaningful KPIs for SCM to measure progress and further improvements.

ANSWERS AND RATIONALE

Question 1 Scenario 1

Question rationale	This question focuses on the value Supplier Management can bring to the Organisation and in being customer-focused and managing opportunities.
MOST CORRECT	C This answer would offer the best potential solution because both organisations would benefit. The organisation would obtain value from a Supplier whose Business strategy was closely aligned to the financial services organisation. A relationship would be forged on mutual trust. The Supplier would benefit because a long-term commitment from the Organisation would lead to financial stability, enabling it to finance longer term investments and deliver value to its customers.

SECOND BEST	B	There is a lot of merit in this answer because the use of preferred suppliers would enable the organisation to spread the risk of sourcing products, and costs could be reduced through competing suppliers. This would also limit or remove the scope for engaging with other suppliers.
THIRD BEST	A	Almost as good as B. Sourcing products through one Supplier may lead to higher costs or delay if the Supplier cannot obtain the goods or services required.
DISTRACTER	D	While the organisation might possibly achieve its objectives, the Contract would be one-sided and no value would be obtained by the Supplier. In the event that a Supplier failed to deliver the products in accordance with the terms of the Contract, the financial penalties imposed might lead to a reduction in service quality or reluctance to provide services on a long-term basis, eventually leading to mistrust and possible termination of Contracts.
Syllabus unit / Module supported		ITIL SC: SOA06 – Supplier Management
Bloom's Taxonomy Testing Level		Level 3 Applying – Use ideas, principles and theories in new, particular and concrete situations. Behavioural tasks at this level involve both knowing and comprehension and might include choosing appropriate procedures, applying principles, using an approach or identifying the selection of options.
		Level 4 Analysis – The ability to use the practices and concepts in a situation or unprompted use of an abstraction. Can apply what is learned in the classroom, in workplace situations. Can separate concepts into component parts to understand structure and can distinguish between facts and inferences.
		Application – The candidate must apply their knowledge of Supplier Management and analyse the stated objectives described in the scenario to select the correct answer option.

Subjects covered	Categories covered:
	• Evaluation of New Suppliers and Contracts
Book section references	SD 4.7.5 – Service Design processes – Supplier Management – Process activities, methods and techniques
	SD 4.7.5.1 – Service Design processes – Supplier Management – Process activities, methods and techniques – Evaluation of new suppliers and contracts
	SD 4.7.5.3 – Service Design processes – Supplier Management – Process activities, methods and techniques – Establishing new suppliers and contracts
	SD 4.7.5.4 – Service Design processes – Supplier Management – Process activities, methods and techniques – Supplier and Contract management and performance
	SD 4.7.5.5 – Service Design processes – Supplier Management – Process activities, methods and techniques – Contract renewal and or termination
Difficulty	Hard

Question 2 Scenario 2

Question rationale	This question focuses on the correct approach to SLM and development of SLAs and OLAs.
MOST CORRECT	A This solution follows the process of Service Level Management. All services that are currently being delivered should be within the Service Catalogue however it is imperative that SLM meet with the business and determine the Service Level Requirement (SLR). Once this requirement has been defined the draft document is produced. During this time existing Operational Level Agreements and contracts should be checked before the signing of the final document.

		Once committed, the service is actively monitored and measured to ensure that IT are meeting the agreed targets.
SECOND BEST	C	Almost as good as A but the document produced should be an SLA not an OLA. Whilst the customer is internal to the organisation, the OLA is between internal suppliers.
THIRD BEST	D	This is not a great way of dealing with the issues. Whilst the aim of maintaining the relationship is present, there may be problems in delivering the levels of service committed to without prior consultation with IT.
DISTRACTER	B	This is almost certainly the reason behind the ill-feeling and distrust. IT should not dictate to the business what level of services they can offer. It is about relationship building and this only comes from negotiation, honesty and communication. This option also confuses SLAs and OLAs.

**Syllabus unit /
Module supported**

ITIL SC: SOA04 – Service Level Management

**Bloom's Taxonomy
Testing Level**

Level 3 Applying – Use ideas, principles and theories in new, particular and concrete situations. Behavioural tasks at this level involve both knowing and comprehension and might include choosing appropriate procedures, applying principles, using an approach or identifying the selection of options.

Level 4 Analysis – The ability to use the practices and concepts in a situation or unprompted use of an abstraction. Can apply what is learned in the classroom, in workplace situations. Can separate concepts into component parts to understand structure and can distinguish between facts and inferences.

Application – The candidate must apply their knowledge of SLM, including the correct process for developing OLAs and SLAs. The candidate must analyse the various options presented and correctly identify the one option which outlines the events in the correct sequence.

Subjects covered Categories covered:

- Service Level Management
- Determining SLRs
- Agreeing SLAs and OLAs

Book section references SD 4.2.5 – Service Design processes – Service Level Management – Process activities, methods and techniques

Difficulty Moderate

Question 3 Scenario 3

Question rationale This question focuses on Return on Investment (ROI) and why a Business Case is important and some of the considerations that need to be taken into account.

MOST CORRECT A This is the most correct answer because it clearly identifies why a Business Case is so important. Also all three common objectives are correct.

SECOND BEST C Good answer, but not as clear as answer A. 2 points are correct, but an increase in reliability is operational and not strategic.

THIRD BEST D Not as good as either A or C, but at least it mentions business objectives. Only 1 answer is under the correct heading. Providing better quality and the introduction of competitive products are strategic.

DISTRACTER B The main reasons for preparing a Business Case have not been addressed. All answers are incorrect. Introducing competitive products is strategic, improving efficiency is operational and improving customer satisfaction is strategic.

Syllabus unit / Module supported ITIL SC: SOA07 – Financial Management

Bloom's Taxonomy Testing Level	Level 3 Applying – Use ideas, principles and theories in new, particular and concrete situations. Behavioural tasks at this level involve both knowing and comprehension and might include choosing appropriate procedures, applying principles, using an approach or identifying the selection of options.
	Level 4 Analysis – The ability to use the practices and concepts in a situation or unprompted use of an abstraction. Can apply what is learned in the classroom, in workplace situations. Can separate concepts into component parts to understand structure and can distinguish between facts and inferences.
	Application – The candidate must apply their content knowledge of ROI and reasons which justify how the business case is important to address the concerns outlined in the scenario.
Subjects covered	Categories covered: • Return on Investment • Business Case
Book section references	SS 5.2.1 – Service Economics – Return On Investment – Business Case
	SS 5.2.1.1 – Service Economics – Return On Investment – Business Case – Business objectives
	SS Table 5.3 – Common Business Objectives
Difficulty	Easy

Question 4 Scenario 4

Question rationale	This question focuses on the challenges associated with Service Catalogue Management.
MOST CORRECT	A This option addresses the issues identified within the scenario and would be a better approach to gaining

		buy in and support to enable a new joint Service Catalogue to be produced, address the need for cultural change and would ensure that an integrated Service Catalogue was brought under control of Change Management.
SECOND BEST	D	While this option has merit and contains many useful activities, there is little integration or interaction with SLM.
THIRD BEST	B	While this option has some merit, a project approach has been adopted and does not address how it will be managed once implemented or address the people and cultural issues.
DISTRACTER	C	This option focuses purely on the technical activities you could undertake.
Syllabus unit / Module supported		ITIL SC: SOA03 – Service Catalogue Management
Bloom's Taxonomy Testing Level		Level 3 Applying – Use ideas, principles and theories in new, particular and concrete situations. Behavioural tasks at this level involve both knowing and comprehension and might include choosing appropriate procedures, applying principles, using an approach or identifying the selection of options.
		Level 4 Analysis – The ability to use the practices and concepts in a situation or unprompted use of an abstraction. Can apply what is learned in the classroom, in workplace situations. Can separate concepts into component parts to understand structure and can distinguish between facts and inferences.
		Application – The candidate must apply their knowledge of SCM and distinguish the best activities from the options that meet the needs described in the scenario and which are consistent with the core guidance.
Subjects covered		Categories covered:

- Service Catalogue Management

Book section references	SD 4.1 – Service Design Processes – Service Catalogue Management
Difficulty	Moderate

INDEX